Kathleen Regan is a writer, mother, and psychiatric nurse with over 30 years' experience. Her memoir is both intense and dramatic as she draws the reader into her family's experiences. She is able to blend her psychiatric expertise with her personal accounts of tragedy, sadness, hope, and resilience. This is, at times, a haunting tale of a troubled child and the author's myriad attempts to master difficult systems to obtain help for her son. She also navigates the complexities of the adoption world and blended families. This honest account narrates her mastery over the emotional turmoil generated by years of crises, through her channeling her energies to help other troubled children and her transition to a calming lifestyle.

Kathleen has previously published a non-fiction book: *Opening Our Arms; Helping Troubled Kids Do Well*, Bull Publishing, Boulder, Co (2006), articles for professional journals, and a variety of pamphlets. She is currently working on a young adult novel.

This book is dedicated to Beth, Andrew, and Mark Tomas.

Kathleen Regan

UNINTENDED CONSEQUENCES

A MOTHER'S MEMOIR

AUSTIN MACAULEY PUBLISHERS™

LONDON • CAMBRIDGE • NEW YORK • SHARJAH

Ordering Information:
Quantity sales: special discounts are available on quantity purchases by corporations, associations, and others. For details, contact the publisher at the address below.

Publisher's Cataloging-in-Publication data
Regan, Kathleen
Unintended Consequences: A Mother's Memoir

ISBN 9781643782362 (Paperback)
ISBN 9781643782379 (Hardback)
ISBN 9781643782386 (Kindle e-book)
ISBN 9781645367246 (ePub e-book)

Library of Congress Control Number: 2019935072

The main category of the book — Family & Relationships / General

www.austinmacauley.com/us

First Published (2019)
Austin Macauley Publishers LLC
40 Wall Street, 28th Floor
New York, NY 10005
USA

mail-usa@austinmacauley.com
+1(646)5125767

I would like to acknowledge the staff of Austin Macauley, without whom this memoir would not exist. I am extremely grateful to my two first readers, both published authors in their own rights. Firstly, I am thankful for my friendship with Carolyn Parkhurst, an acclaimed fiction novelist. Her support and suggestions led to a richer manuscript with more emotional depth. Ellen Ratner, a recognized non-fiction author who was not only my friend, former boss, and a make-it-happen dynamo, but also perceptive, and her suggestions in showing parallels between my personal experiences and my professional life in generating changes for humane care for children made the manuscript clearer and more finely knitted. It was under her tutelage in my early career that I came into my own and developed a sense of competence and confidence.

I am also extremely thankful and blessed for my staff at the Child Assessment Unit. Together we did great things for a large number of troubled youngsters and their families over a thirteen-year period. I am appreciative of all the Psychiatric Nurse Leaders and Program Directors who were supportive of the innovations we initiated. They visited us and observed us in action on the unit and then went back to their units and programs to move forward in more humane care of children. Most importantly, our endeavors were in large part due to Dr. Ross Greene. His brilliant approach to managing and understanding explosive children laid our foundation and was the framework around which we built our model of humane care of children.

I am grateful for the friends who supported me and watched over me during the years of acute crisis—Kathy, Debbie, Heidi, and Chris, all helped me through difficult times. I also credit my fantastic friends from Adoptive Families Together. They provided my education of the complex issues of adoption, and their strength in the midst of their own crises was inspiring. My college roommate and later-life friend Doreen was instrumental in supporting my move and welcoming me to my new home in Florida. Lastly, I am fortunate to have found friends who were welcoming—to all my VR buddies, you helped me find peace and made my lifestyle transition much easier than I had thought possible.

My gratefulness extends above all to my parents, who instilled in me a sense of social justice and their parenting gave me an inner strength upon which to draw from in difficult times and enabled my persistence and resilience.

Table of Contents

Chapter 1
March 2014:
A Tragedy Unfolds

I was volunteering at my church, folding flyers for the coming Sundays mass. It was Friday, March 14, 2014; at about 10 o'clock in the morning when my cell phone rang.

I answered it to hear my ex-brother-in-law, Bernie, say, "Hello, Kathy. This is Bernie."

I wondered why he was calling me, but I simply responded: "Hi, Bernie."

Bernie then said: "Are you alone?" *Stranger still*, I thought.

I responded, "No, I'm at my church, folding flyers. Why?"

Bernie went on to say: "Find a place where you are alone and sit down."

Wow, I still have no clue what this is all about. I walked into a nearby meeting room, closed the door, and took a seat on one of the couches. "OK, Bernie, what's up?"

Bernie then related, "Kathy, Mark has died." Before I could ask how and what was the medical cause, Bernie went on to tell me, "Mark was found this morning, and it appears that he was shot several times. The police are here at the house and Mark Tomas is being taken in for questioning. The TV crews are arriving so you need to call Beth and Andy right away before this is on the news."

I felt dazed, numb, in shock maybe, but I knew I had to call my children right away. I called Beth and also told her to sit down. Then I reported: "Beth, Bernie just called me. Your father has died. I'm so sorry, honey. He told me that Mark was found with several gunshot wounds and Mark Tomas was being taken in for questioning. He said that a lot of police were at the house and TV crews were arriving. I'm leaving now to go home. Can you come over now?"

Beth was crushed and crying but said she would leave work and would call Bernie for more details before she drove to my home. Next I called my son, Andy, at his work in another state and relayed the same horrible news. He was also upset and crying, and said he too would call his uncle for more details. Mark Tomas was my eldest child and he was now thirty-four years of age. Andy followed two years later, so he was now almost thirty-two, and Beth was born in 1986, so she was about to turn twenty-eight years old.

I left the church and drove home. Luckily, it was in the next town, only a few miles away. I was able to take local roads and did not have to deal with traffic. I do not remember driving home, but I entered my home and sat down. That did not work, so I got up and began pacing around the room. I lost all sense of time that day. And I don't know if Beth arrived in an hour or if it was two or three hours later. Beth had been in contact with both Bernie and Andy and had learned more information in the course of that day. As she filled me in with details, it was frustrating to her that I couldn't seem to hold on to the information she was telling me.

I would ask the same questions over and over. She finally suggested that I take something to calm my nerves. I did take an Ativan 0.5milligram pill to see if it would help in making me feel less dazed and foggy. This was the death of my ex-husband. But he had been my husband for thirty-one years. He was the most significant person in my adult life. And in the first decade of our marriage, we had been happy as life partners. He was the father of my children. We had so much history together, some happy, some sad. And we had agonized, together and separately, about our oldest son. Now I was alone, trying to be a support to my two children who had lost their father. And as a mother, I was trying to come to terms with the nightmare and my very worst fears coming true: my son having committed some terrible act which would likely result in a life-long prison term.

Over the course of the next thirty-six hours, more details emerged as Beth had multiple conversations, as did Andy. The story was covered on the TV news. This event took place on a

Friday, but it started unfolding on Tuesday of that week. Mark did not show up for work at FedEx. It was a job he loved and he was seldom out sick. Not showing up without a phone call was uncharacteristic. Tuesday evening, a coworker went to his home and reported that Mark Tomas answered the door and stated that his father was not home, and he did not know where he was. Mark's coworkers were doubly concerned when he did not show up on Wednesday. Mark's boss at FedEx called Mark's brother (who was listed as his contact person on his employment forms) to express his concern.

Shortly thereafter, a couple of Mark's relatives went to the house and knocked on the door, but there was no response. Later that day, they contacted the police for a wellness check, and Bernie accompanied a police officer to the home. Again, there was no answer, but they noted that Mark's car was in front of the home. At this point, both the police officer and Bernie were suspicious. Mark's family knew from statements their brother had made that he was living in a potentially dangerous situation and they had advised him of their concern.

On Friday, Mark's brother, Bernie, and a police officer did a second wellness check. Again, there was no response to their knocking on the door. On wellness checks, there can be no forced entry. Now very concerned, they observed that a window on the second floor appeared to be open. The officer obtained a ladder and was able to enter the home from the second story window. Once inside, Mark was located in his bedroom, on the floor. He was deceased, and multiple gunshot wounds were evident. The officer called in what he had found and shortly thereafter, other officers arrived.

A search of the house was done, and Mark Tomas was found hiding in the attic. He was uncommunicative and had a strange look on his face. He was handcuffed and taken into custody for questioning. After twenty-four hours of questioning Mark Tomas, interviewing neighbors, as well as evidence found in the home, the family was notified that Mark Tomas would remain in custody and that he was being arrested. He was charged with murder one, a capital offence. This occurred on Friday afternoon. This is the chain of events as I recall them. I can't attest to their total accuracy as I was receiving

13

information third-hand, so there may be slightly different versions of who did what and when.

The next few days were filled with learning information about and planning for the wake and funeral. Both events were beyond difficult. I wanted to be a support to my children, and they wanted me there with them. I did not feel this was the time for me to be grieving for what might have been since the events around Mark's death were so traumatic. It was awkward at times as Mark had been my husband for over thirty years, but we had divorced six years prior and I had had almost no contact with his brothers and sisters since that time.

Bernie was the point person on all the arrangements and he updated Andy and Beth as arrangements were made. I stood with Andy and Beth at the wake and beside them at the funeral and burial. At the wake, I was surprised to see how many of my friends and how many of my adoptive support network friends had come to offer me support and condolences. The women understood that beyond the loss of my once husband, I was the mother of the person accused of murdering him. I cried for all of us and I cried for Mark Tomas.

For those few days, my home was not peaceful. Andy had arrived with his family and Beth with her partner. There was much crying and friends of both of my adult children were streaming in and out to show their support.

I was used to a quiet life, so all this activity and the intensity of all the emotions was stressful and it left me feeling wired rather than comforted. After the funeral, my children returned to their homes and we shared news about Mark Tomas as anyone received it from Mark's family.

Finally, we heard that the arraignment had been scheduled. Beth came to my home the night before to drive me to the courthouse. It was winter in New England so we were bundled up in winter coats and gloves. We entered the courthouse and at the lobby information desk, we asked directions for the arraignment hearing. We were directed up a flight of stairs to a large lobby area. Here I spotted many of Mark's family. His sisters and his sisters-in-law were friendly and welcoming, which put me somewhat at ease. We were all here for a tragic event. I think that Mark's brothers had a more difficult time figuring out my place as they were so angry at the loss of their brother and at Mark Tomas for causing this tragedy. My being his mother and my having divorced their brother, I think, created a lot of ambivalence for them.

As in most court sessions, it was a 'hurry up and wait' scenario. The DA's office staff met with the family and walked them through what was likely to occur that morning and explained that since the charge was capital one murder, the actual trial was at least two years down the road. Today's arraignment was the start of a long process.

Finally, we were directed to a particular courtroom where the arraignment was to take place. I sat with Beth and with the Regan family as we waited for Mark Tomas' name to be called. As I looked around the courtroom, I noticed that two of Mark's cousins, who were on the Boston Police Force, were in attendance at the back of the room. I also spotted a TV cameraman at the rear of the room.

Mark Tomas' name was called and he entered through a side door to sit with his court-appointed lawyer at the defense table. He kept his head down, was in an orange jump suit, and was shackled at the wrists. He made no attempt to glance around the courtroom as he entered the room nor did he attempt to look around once seated. I was able to catch a glimpse of the side of his face from one of the large side mirrors situated atop the door he had entered.

Here I was, sitting in a courtroom watching the proceedings as my son was arraigned for the murder of his father and my husband for thirty-one years. We had raised him and loved him, and here I was in this courtroom, thinking about what had happened to our lives that resulted in bringing us to this point.

Chapter 2
1968: Starting Out

I graduated from Stonehill College in June of 1968 and it was an exciting time to be living in. Our generation was questioning norms, breaking rules, and protesting what they felt were wrong decisions made by those in authority. I had been raised by liberal parents who instilled in all three of their children a sense of social justice. At our dinner table while growing up, there were not only conversations about how our day had gone, but we discussed what was happening in our country and in a broader sense, the larger world. While my parents were outspoken, we were encouraged to contribute to the conversation and give reasons for our views.

I found that when I arrived at Stonehill College, a Catholic liberal arts college in New England, my views were more liberal than the majority of the student body. In fact, many of our teachers, who were Holy Cross priests, were also more liberal than the majority of students. Stonehill was a small school located about twenty miles outside of Boston and over 50 percent of the student body were commuters. For some unknown reason, a number of high school graduates from my small town of Brewster, NY, landed at this college in Massachusetts over the past decade. Those of us who were boarders made close friendships and spent a lot of time together.

I used to muse sometimes that some of the faculty had more radical views, even about Catholicism, than I had anticipated. As I was sociology major, there were ample opportunities to question how and why things happened, the moral implications of decision-making, and its effect on others. And those years were ripe for discussions such as these.

Since the curriculum required minors in Philosophy and Theology, this meant that every semester, we took one of each of those courses along with other liberal arts requirements and the courses of our chosen major. Our courses, by their very nature, directed our thinking philosophically, ethically, and spiritually. I felt I had really grown in this environment and had come into my own there. Contextually, it was the 60s and the world was shaking with this generation as it questioned and refused to accept the status quo. I had a boyfriend from my senior year, Phil, who was considered to be radical in his views, and we had many discussions about what would be our involvement in shaping the changes that were occurring.

He came from Irish Catholic parents who lived on the south shore, not far from campus. He was anti-business, which I think was influenced by his father having some business setbacks while Phil was younger and living at home. It soured him on the business sector and influenced his views on 'the establishment'. I found him to be attractive and very bright and I was surprised and pleased that he was attracted to me. I was flattered at his enjoying conversations with me where we questioned and developed opinions on a number of issues.

Many of the courses in junior and senior year required end-of-the-semester term papers and despite not liking the concurrent deadlines, I discovered that I liked putting my thoughts to paper. I learned that I had a skill in writing things down and working out solutions by putting pen to paper. I also found that one of my favorite courses was Logic and that my mind was drawn to logical, clear, concise thinking.

Two of my roommates shared apartments with me for all four years. Our fourth roommate varied between a couple of women at various times. We lived off-campus in various apartments during our four years as Stonehill did not, at that time, have on-campus dorms for women. As roommates, we spent a lot of time together and frequently socialized together in the evenings and on campus for various activities. My first three years were spent on campus or locally, but in my senior year, dating Phil, we frequently went into Boston on weekends.

I also spent several weekends at his parent's home, which was in a suburb south of Boston and about fifteen miles from the college. His parents were good people who welcomed me into their home. His father worked in real estate and I do not remember where his mother worked. They had three children, Phil was the oldest, followed by Jim and his younger sister, Marilyn. Neither parent had had the opportunity to attend college, but they were bright and had been very successful. They had lived in a tiny suburb, Darien, Connecticut for a number of years before returning to their home state of Massachusetts. I enjoyed the weekends I spent at their home.

My four years at Stonehill seemed to have slid by, but in that four years, I developed close friendships, learned to cook on a meager budget, learned to play Whisk (an old-fashioned card game that was a precursor to Bridge but was much easier), learned how to communicate my views, and become more articulate. I found that in those four years, I became an independent person with strong opinions.

I remember during Freshman Orientation Week, we had a speech delivered by the President of the College. He said: "Look around you to the person sitting on your left and on your right. Out of the three of you, only one of you will be here on graduation day." I thought to myself: *I think I heard that right. I hope I'm the one here in four years. What a sobering thought.* I genuinely wasn't sure that I had heard him correctly.

He had a strong New England accent and I was trying to figure out what people were saying to me that first month. But here I was four years later, graduating and about to begin my first full-time professional job. I had taken the Massachusetts State exam for Social Worker, had passed it, and had had an interview prior to graduation. I was told I would be given a job that would start July 1, 1968, but I would only learn to which office I had been assigned two weeks prior to the starting date.

After a few weeks of resting at home, I started to prepare for my new life. I packed what I would need immediately after moving away and what I would like to have with me once I was settled. My new job required a car and my parents cosigned the loan for my first new automobile. It was a Chevy Nova.

Mid-June, the letter arrived officially, informing me of my acceptance as an employee for the Department of Social Services in the Child Guardianship Division and that I had been assigned to an office in Brocton. I packed my new car and set out to Boston to look for temporary lodging. Not knowing the area, I initially found myself responding to rooming house ads in some very dangerous neighborhoods in Roxbury and Mattapan. After a few days, I obtained a room in a rooming house in Brookline. I needed to save some money before I could think about signing a lease for an apartment and have the necessary deposits.

As the state was having budget problems, a freeze had been put on additional spending. So, my position and all the new hires as of that July, 1968, were told to begin work, but we would not be paid until the budget crisis had resolved. That crisis lasted over seven weeks, so I relied on my parents funding me until I began to draw a salary. Now, mind you, this was 1968 and my starting salary was $6,000 a year. And for that measly annual salary of $6,000, I inherited a caseload of seventy-two foster children and six unwed mothers.

The caseload had been uncovered for the past year, following the exit of the previous caseworker who had left the agency. On my first week on the job, three very frustrated foster moms called me to state that they were done and that their respective foster children needed to be picked on Friday by 3 pm. My first supervisor had his feet up on the desk, reading a non-work-related magazine, when I entered frantically asking: "What am I going to do?"

His response was: "Check on any relatives of those kids and see if they would be willing to take them."

I responded: "Well, I know one of the children has a relative in Colorado."

His response: "I'll authorize you making an out-of-state call to them." I couldn't believe it!

I spent the first three months of that job calling my mother several times a week at night for advice. I was a third-generation social worker and my mom had many years' social work experience. In fact, at that point in time, she was the Chief of Probation for Putnam County, NY. She started her practice as a social worker for the City of New York Department of Welfare. She gave me practical advice such as, "Go see the foster families who were upset with the agency and find out as much information as you can from them about their experience and about the behaviors of the children for whom they no longer feel able to care". Her advice and my quick following of it at least gave me some lead-time to find other foster homes. What a beginning for my first professional job.

I worked four years at this job and learned much about the foster care system, its problems, and the politics that surrounded it. I became a volunteer union representative where we advocated for tolerable caseloads, more qualified supervisors, and better pay. Much as I cared for most of the children in my caseload, I knew I would have no future in this job. My biggest and most influencing challenge was that I did not have it in me to play God.

At times, that was exactly what my role felt like. I remember, distinctly having a case where a young couple who were impoverished and illiterate had two young children, a baby under a year and a toddler. They were living in an apartment in a city south of Boston. I was trying to provide child guidance to the mom. The father was rarely home when I visited, as his wife reported to me that he was out, looking for work. A child abuse and neglect complaint had been filed and had been screened in as needing the department's oversight. I became increasingly concerned with the lack of progress and felt the home situation was deteriorating.

The house was filthy, the children often found in dirty diapers, and little food was apparent. Even when the children were crying, the mom repeatedly needed direction to pick up and cuddle with the baby and the toddler. After nine months of making no headway, I let the mom know that there was a chance their children would be removed from the home if she and her husband were unable to show more consistent care for their children. The deciding factor was another complaint called into the office by a neighbor reporting that the mother had gone out leaving the children alone and had not returned for several hours.

After I had given my warning, all cooperation ceased. There was no answer to my phone messages and when I arrived for a visit, no one was home; or if they were home, no one answered the door. Then the agency received several phone calls from anonymous neighbors and from a pediatrician's office that the children were not being brought in for exams and for their vaccinations.

My supervisor consulted with the agency attorney and I was told it was time for me to write a care and custody petition for the court and that the agency would bring the case before a judge for a decision regarding the state taking over care and custody of the children. I agonized over the petition and worked on it for two weeks. My supervisor read the report and signed off on it. Then the report was sent to the agency court attorney. He had only minor changes for me but had specific wording that he wanted placed in the conclusion of the report. A hearing date was scheduled for the County Probate Court. The attorney met with me to prepare me for testifying before the judge regarding the accuracy of my report. The report had been sent to the juvenile department in the Probate Court several weeks prior to the scheduled hearing.

I had a friend, Chris, with whom I worked and I asked her to accompany me to the court hearing. I was very anxious and felt an awful sense of responsibility. The report was over twelve pages and detailed the state of the children's care over the past nine months and steps to ameliorate their care and the parents' response to the suggestions and the treatment plan. The conclusion was on the last page in which I had stated that despite the efforts of the department (me), no progress was occurring and the children were at risk and needed temporary placement in a home that was capable of providing the care they deserved and needed.

Chris and I arrived at the courthouse at about 9 am, and I did not see the parents in the lobby. An hour later, the parents arrived with both children in their arms. They greeted me warily. The case was finally called and we entered the courtroom. The court officer called the case and directed Chris and me to one side of the court and the parents to a table on the other side of the judge's bench. Since this was a juvenile custody issue, the courtroom was closed to the public. The judge was handed my report by the clerk; he opened it and immediately turned to the last page and read the conclusion. He did not even glance at the previous eleven pages. I was flabbergasted and underneath that, I felt resentful.

He turned to me and asked if the report was accurate. I answered yes. Then he turned to the parents and asked if they had anything to say. The parents nodded no. The judge looked

21

at the children and made some disparaging remarks about the parents' poor care of the children. He then looked up and remanded the children to the care of the Division of Child Guardianship (DCG) for temporary custody for the next six months at which time, a determination would be made to either return the children to their home or for Permanent Custody to be transferred to the DCG.

Chris and I walked out of the courtroom to the hall and a court officer walked up to the parents and told them to give the children to both of us. The parents complied and placed the two children in both of our arms. They walked out the door dry-eyed, and Chris and I walked out of the courthouse crying with a child in each of our arms. I never forgot that day, the judge did not even read the report. He just turned to the conclusion. I left feeling he may have been the judge, but I felt like I was the one making the decision. And it was playing God, I didn't like the feeling at all.

Chapter 3
My Early 20s and My Short-Lived First Marriage

On a personal front, I was making changes in my own life. Attending college had been formative and definitely had me flexing my brain muscles in examining my beliefs. I was also forging my identity as a person. And the four years at college left me with a clearer sense of who I was in general and I was comfortable in thinking about who I thought I was. I had increased my confidence level and recognized my ability to identify problems and find solutions that I thought worked for me. This was consistent with the image of myself I had grown up with. My mother would state matter-of-factly that my brother, Tony, was the really bright one; my sister, Patty, was the creative one, and I was the child with the most common sense.

As a teenager, I thought I was getting the shorter end of the stick compared to my siblings' talents, but my mother thought she was complementing me and would add that she and my dad could rely on me as they trusted my judgment. Now as an adult, I could see that talents didn't necessarily involve an either/or dispersion. By my senior year, I had discovered that I was smart and that I was able to make decisions easily and that my decision-making was grounded in assessing and considering alternatives that were sound despite being quickly formed. I had discovered that I had an organized and logical mind and that I had an ability to see the larger picture when examining an issue. While I had several boyfriends over that four years, my senior year, I dated Phil, and this relationship seemed more serious. We made plans to live together once we had both found established jobs.

The rooming house in Brookline where I was staying was a suburb of Boston and about 20 miles from my office in Brockton, Ma. It was tolerably clean but old with no fixings. My room was bare, with a bed and a dresser. The bathroom was at the end of the hall and was for all the residents on that floor. There was no lock on the bathroom door, and I vividly remember bringing my suitcase into the bathroom and pushing it upright against the door when I went to shower in the evenings. I shared the floor with three older men, only one of which I would run into in the hallway on a regular basis.

Living in that rooming house made me feel like I was a transient person and I knew I never wanted to feel at loose ends requiring me to live in a place like that again. I had a roof over my head, but that was all I had. I wanted to move out of there as soon as was possible. Phil and I had made plans to get an apartment together, as soon as his employment was squared away. His situation was more complicated than mine. The draft was in full swing for the Vietnam War and he had a low lottery number. He was strongly opposed to the war.

At the start of his senior year, he had applied for Conscientious Objector status and was awaiting a hearing. He also had one or two courses, which he needed to complete that summer before obtaining his degree. His draft hearing took place in early July, pending his finding a job that met the criteria for CO work. He was granted this status and was required to spend the next two years in this capacity. He obtained a job at Project Place, a shelter for run-away adolescents in the South End section of Boston. By September 15, we had moved into a one-bedroom attic apartment in Cambridge, Ma.

We married the following February of 1969 in my hometown of Brewster, New York. We had a Catholic wedding in the local church followed by a small reception in a nearby town at a restaurant, called Dreamwald. The weekend of our wedding, it snowed and a number of our Boston friends were unable to attend. Our honeymoon was a long weekend in Rockport, Massachusetts in an Inn on the ocean.

In retrospect, Phil and I would have been better off to have lived together and not been in a rush to marry. I think I felt pressured by my parents who, while not being overly critical, were not comfortable with my living with a man and not being married. Phil and I felt we loved each other, so we went into the marriage with not a lot of forethought.

And it worked for a time—less than eighteen months. But problems emerged quickly. In somewhat egalitarian fashion, we decided that everything needed to be shared fifty-fifty. In reality, it didn't work. First of all, I did all the cooking while Phil did the dishes. I did most of the cleaning, but truth be told, the apartment was so small, there wasn't a lot to clean. But bill paying was a much larger issue. When it was my month to pay the bills, I would see that they were overdue. I learned that Phil resented having to pay bills and would put them off and delay doing them, so it fell on my months to get things straightened out.

But we had a lot of good times together too, in the initial stages. Despite my having a responsible job as a social work for the state, our free time was spent in a hippie-like lifestyle. We gathered with friends, listened to music, smoked pot, and went to protest marches and rallies. We even had several occasions where we planned to 'trip' together with friends taking either LSD or MDA, both hallucinogens that were readily available at that time.

On one occasion, Phil and I and another couple took MDA and decided to drive to the Cape and experience nature on the sand dunes of Provincetown. When we had almost reached our destination, the car in front of us hit the car before it. We stopped in time, and the collision resulted in auto damage, but no one was hurt. Being under the influence of the drug, I experienced the crash in slow motion, and the vision repeated itself over and over until I was getting really upset. By then, we had reached the dunes and everyone worked hard at distracting me and putting me in a better emotional place. They were successful and we spent the day on the dunes talking, picnicking, and listening to music.

Another time, we were with this same couple in Boston and had taken LSD at their apartment. The other man suggested we see the city from a beautiful view and he led us to this point. We had to climb a ladder, which was attached to the side of the building and arrived on this enormous flat roof that overlooked the city from several vantage points. We were oohing and aahhing over the different views when all of a sudden, men starting appearing on the roof from several different directions. As they got closer, we could see that they were policemen, and there were over ten of them coming towards us. Before I had time to get really scared, one officer said to the others, "Let me handle this. They are tripping." The officer approached and said calmly but firmly, "Do you know where you are? You are on the roof of the Copley Shopping Plaza and there are three banks under you. You have triggered alarms on all of them."

We apologized and stated we did not know that the shopping center was beneath us. He then said, "I want you leave now and you are to never return here." He walked us to the nearest ladder and we descended. When we reached the street, we quickly made it around the corner and returned to the other couple's apartment. Thankfully, it was the '60s. In this day and age, we would have been arrested on several Federal charges and it would have been the end of any chance of a successful career.

We went to Woodstock and reveled in the mud and listened to great music for three days and most of three nights. We went with our friends Fitz and Gail. The party started before we arrived. Cars were backed up for miles trying to get into the festival sight and folks got on top of their cars and blasted car music while waiting for the bottleneck to clear. The atmosphere was festive and communal. Everyone shared food and joints. The Hog Farmer's Commune set up tents to help people who were having 'bad trips' and they also fed people who arrived and came unprepared.

We were able to hear fantastic bands. What was as striking as the great music was witnessing a phenomenon where people came together and were genuinely caring to one another. And we were all strangers. We were bathing in a lake on the farm's property since the rain had turned the site to mud, and going back and forth to the porta potties entailed sliding in the mud and being covered in it by the end of each day. Everyone shared joints and passed them around. We had brought supplies, so we had a cooler, which the guys lugged back and forth each day from the campsite to the music area grounds. We brought sandwiches, soda, snacks and candy.

We shared what we had with those around us. Joints were passed up and down the rows of people on blankets. The very air was filled with the aroma of marijuana. You could have gotten a contact high without ever lighting a joint. We sat on blankets in the grass (mud) and listened to music twelve hours or more a day. We watched the helicopters land near the staging area and then an announcement would be made about which famous band had just arrived. Some people gave up wearing clothes due to all the mud. Needless to say, our group of four was not in that camp! But we did have to rinse out our clothes and air-dry them when we got back to our tent.

During the '60s and early '70s, everything was more flexible and much less rigid and regimented than is the case now. I was allowed to save my three weeks' vacation time allotted to me after my first year of employment. And when the next July arrived, having gotten the approval from my boss, I was allowed to take the six weeks' vacation as paid leave, as I had now worked a full two years. For the previous eighteen months, Phil and I and our friends, Fitz and Gail, met regularly to plan a six-week camping trip across America.

When we got together, we would assign tasks in preparation for the trip. We planned to take Fitz's van. He was a sculptor of very large acrylic abstract pieces, so he required a large van in order to transport them from one site to another. He built shelves along the inner sides of the van, which would be used for storing cans and dried goods for the trip. It served as our built-in pantry. He also built platforms for beds that would lift down from the ceiling at night for sleeping but could be lifted back up and hooked in place during the day. This allowed space for seating when traveling during the day. Gail and I worked on developing a file box of index cards listing meals with ingredients and directions, which could be cooked over an open fire.

Phil was in charge of researching our routes cross-country and back, and for presenting us with possible sights to see upon which we would vote and make decisions. Once we voted and the decisions were made, he would map out the routes we would travel. Another task we undertook together was to take two large boxes of Tampax and transform them as marijuana suppositories. The guys would roll the joints, and Gail and I

27

would carefully remove the tampon from the paper wrapper. Then we would empty the cardboard tampon cartridge of the tampon itself. Next, we would take three jumbo joints the guys had rolled and insert them in the cardboard cylinder and put the cartridge back in the paper wrapper and twist the very end and place its twisted side down back in the Tampax box. That was to be stored strategically in the luggage area of the van. After a year and a half of planning, we started out.

The trip was a wonderful experience. We took the northern route to the West Coast and the Southern Route back to the East Coast. We had great weather and were able to sleep under the stars in sleeping bags all but four days of the six weeks of the trip. We cooked over the campfire at night and we traveled by day. We camped out in wheat fields in the Midwest, and on the beaches on the West Coast. We drove through the Rockies and part of our trip followed that of Ken Kesey and his Merry Pranksters.

We showered in state parks and bathed in open rivers. We saw first-hand much of the beauty of our country. We saw the Grand Canyon, Little Bighorn, Yellowstone Park, the Grand Sequoias, Montana, Utah, Washington and Oregon, Big Sur, the Badlands, Arizona, New Mexico, Memphis, New Orleans, Georgia. We were stopped numerous times in the South, since we looked like a bunch of hippies in a van. We were not a welcome sight to local law enforcement. Each and every time our van was searched for drugs, we would watch as the local or state police tenuously lifted the boxes of Tampax and moved them to the side while they searched our luggage and the van for contraband!

We visited several of the more well-known communes at the time and that lifestyle appealed more to Phil than it did to me. Some of them had no electricity or indoor plumbing, and I had no desire to lead that rustic a life. My dismissal of places that were so primitive as to be unlivable was a cause of contention between us.

We were better at having fun than being serious. And discussions, as we traveled, that centered on our future were harbingers of fissures that would become more apparent when we returned to our everyday lives.

Shortly after our return from our trip, I remember a visit home to my parents. Over the course of what started out as a political discussion, it deteriorated and became personal. It got very heated and Phil made some very disparaging remarks about my mother. I became upset and went into the bedroom and packed up our suitcase and told Phil we were leaving. I could see my father was furious and at that point, both my mother and I were crying. I left feeling like I was being pressured to choose sides and I had no desire to do so. On some level, I sensed a bridge had been crossed whether or not I was ready for it to be crossed.

Within a few months, things came to a head when Phil began to question whether or not we should have an 'open marriage', committed yet able to date others. 'Dating others' was a euphemism for sleeping with others and I had no interest in that concept at all. When it became obvious to me that he was serious, I began to talk of a trial separation. Things moved quickly as I became aware of one of his female co-workers at Project Place was hanging around our apartment too frequently. We had, at this time, moved into an apartment directly above Project Place, in the South End district of Boston. I would return home from work to find her in the apartment.

The handwriting was on the wall and I began looking in a local community paper for ads of young people who were looking for roommates. I responded to one ad and met with two single working women in their 20s and a male friend of theirs. They were looking for a fourth roommate. The interview went well and they were accepting of my reason for wanting to share an apartment. Within a week, I was separated and had moved my meager belongings into this apartment in Boston in the Copley Square area. I lived with Judy and Mary for over the next three plus years and they became good friends in that phase of my life.

At work, Chris had become a good friend and we socialized after work on a regular basis. She was a couple of years younger than me, but she had already lost her father to cancer. Her mother also died at an early age and she raised her younger sister during her sister's teen years. Chis was smart, fun to be around and we found that not only did we have a lot in common, but we genuinely enjoyed each other's company. She, like myself, did not envision a long career at the Division of Child Guardianship. The following summer, we decided to take a trip together backpacking around parts of Europe for three-plus weeks. It felt like a good way to get over my heartache and concentrate on something other than what I felt was my disaster of a marriage.

We had bought the book: *Europe on Five Dollars a Day* and used it as our guide for food and pensions. The pensions where we would stay cost $4.00 a night. And we would pay an additional 25 cents if we wanted a hot shower, as opposed to a cold shower, which was often included in the price of the room. Most of the pensions were homes or apartments owned by widows. By renting out rooms by the night, they were able to maintain and have money for the upkeep of their homes.

Just before I left, I wrote a note to my parents. Phil and I had been separated for several months and I was anxious about letting them know we had separated. I didn't want to discuss it with them for fear that they might say what I considered terrible things about Phil. And I was not yet sure if this separation was temporary or a genuine ending. I wanted room to navigate my future without the people I was closest to being adamantly opposed to each other.

Even more worrisome to me was that I had separated from my husband and I was fearful that my parents would be upset that I was jeopardizing my Catholic marriage. They were traditional Catholics and that meant for better or for worst, therefore, my place was with Phil. In my letter to them, I asked them to wait five weeks before responding to the letter. I also told them of my new living situation and my address and phone number. Last of all, I told them of my upcoming trip to Europe, with my girlfriend, Chris, and that they should not worry about me. I would send them postcards from our various destinations.

My mother called me as soon as they received the letter. She wanted to let me know that they were glad I was safe. She had been worried by my silence and very vague comments when I had made a few phone calls to them over the past months. She also informed me that she and my father were not angry with me, in fact, they were relieved that I had separated. That last comment caught me by surprise. I felt we had much to discuss at a later time, but I could now take off for my vacation without worrying about their reaction to my news.

Chris and I jam-packed as much as we could in our trek around parts of Europe. And we jam-packed all our belongings for the trip into one backpack each—and that included rolls of American toilet paper!!! Our routine was to get up in the morning, shower, and be out for the day. We would have coffee and bread or pastry for breakfast and shop at local markets for bread, cheese, and wine for a lunchtime picnic at some park in whatever city we were in. We went out to dinner at night at local restaurants listed in our guide or went to places recommended by people we met in each city.

In between meals and after dinner, we walked through cities and saw as many sights as we could pack in day by day. We experienced many of the at-the-time typical experiences. We were pinched on the bum in Rome several times, yelled at on the Metro in France by a woman who objected to our asking directions in English, and we were asked if we would talk with Spanish young men who wanted to practice their English. Our most important items proved to be our shoes. We walked, we toured, we walked our way through Europe. In Italy, I found a pair of cork and leather wedge sandals and they were my salvation from blisters and sore feet.

In Italy, we landed in Rome and traveled from Rome to Florence, and Venice. At the Rome airport, we met an Indian man in his thirties while we were waiting for our luggage. He had been working in Rome for over a year and he offered to accompany us to a local restaurant that was frequented by natives in the area. We met him at 7 pm that evening, and he took us to an unmarked basement restaurant where we had a wonderful meal. There was no menu. The husband and wife bought fresh local food in the morning at the market and prepared the same meal for everyone they served that evening.

It was a great introduction to Rome. We saw the Coliseum and the Roman Forum. We took motorcycle rides, riding shotgun with two young Italian men that was hair-raising but resulted in a splendid panorama of the city, looking down from the hills outside of Rome. We viewed the Trevi Fountain and climbed the Spanish Steps. We toured the Vatican and the Vatican Museum. In Saint Peter's Cathedral, we saw the Pieta.

We walked through Rome but did use the buses on one or two occasions.

In Florence, we toured churches with great artwork and architecture. Sometimes, several of these beautiful churches were located within the same square or piazza. We saw the de Medici gardens. Although Florence was a city, its sights were all within walking distance and we walked back and forth for miles each day. We saw the Uffizi Gallery and walked across Ponte Vecchio. We saw the Piazza del Duomo, the Church of Santa Maria Novella, and the Florence Cathedral. In the Galleria dell'Academia, we were awed by Michelangelo's sculpture of David.

Our next stop via Eurail was Venice. I adored Venice for its beautiful buildings and plazas, canals, and great meals. We took a gondola on the Grand Canal. We ate at outdoor cafés in the evening and people-watched all the bustling activity around us in Piazza San Marco. We viewed the Doge's Palace, St. Mark's Basilica, and the Galleria dell'Academia.

We took the boat to the isle of Murano to see the glassblowers. I bought my parents a set of Green crystal hand blown glasses from there, and Chris and I each purchased a hand-blown lamp.

We then took the Eurail to Paris where we spent three days. It was a beautiful but large, sprawled-out city, and we relied heavily on the Metro to transport us around from site to site. After having been yelled at by the Parisian woman on the train, we were glad to find that the metro maps were very clear and interactive. They got us from place to place. We saw the Arc de Triomphe and the Eiffel Tower. We spent hours in The Louvre. We walked the Champs Elysees. We strolled through the Versailles gardens and had our picnic lunch there as we also did another day at the Garden des Tuileries. We toured the Notre Dame de Paris, the Musée d'Orsay, the Palace Royale, and the Petit Palace.

Next, we traveled to Marseilles. This was a confusing city and more of a melting pot than any other place we traveled. There were neighborhoods of former residents of many African countries side by side, separated by only one block from another. It was crowded and bubbling with life, but it was a little scary, too. It was a hubbub of waterfront shipping activity.

The next stop involved again taking the Eurail through France to the Spanish border. Here we had to depart while the rail cars were switched to fit the rails for Spain. We re-embarked and traveled on to Barcelona. We stayed two days in Barcelona and fell in love with the food there. We met a man who took us on a tour of local vermouth makers. They had their shops in cellars, and we were given samples of their own vermouth with cheese tidbits.

While in Barcelona, we walked the street where Picasso had lived, and we saw Joan Miró paintings. We found a restaurant called 'Kit Kat'. We loved the food there so much that we ate there each evening and when we returned after a day away, we ate there a third time. We took the train down to the Gold Coast of Spain where many wealthy foreigners were purchasing oceanfront properties and building gorgeous homes or mansions. We saw Marabella's black sand beach. We returned to Barcelona for a day and then retraced our path on the train back to Paris and switched trains to travel to London.

We spent about four days in London. Here our guidebook made an error. The address listed for the pension did not exist and as we stopped, looking puzzled, a young woman with an infant in tow, exited her flat and asked if she could help us. We showed her our guidebook with the pension address listed and she confirmed that the information was inaccurate. She and her baby had red curly ringlets for hair. She was friendly and very trusting as she offered up her apartment for us to stay while in London. We did stay with her and she had made a key for us so we could come and go as we pleased. She wanted no money from us despite the fact that she was clearly on a limited budget and receiving welfare while on her maternity leave.

We used her flat as our home base, but we would leave early in the morning and return late in the evening to sleep. An interesting tidbit here was that she relayed she suffered a bout of post-partum depression after the birth of her daughter. She showed me the prescribed medication her doctor had ordered. I was genuinely surprised. It was a jar of black tincture of hashish, prescription label and all! Also, it was interesting to note that the social service agency the government assigned to her was The Daughters of Bilitis, a lesbian social service group.

Here England was light years ahead of where things were in the US in terms of social inclusion. When we left four days later, she was already out for an appointment with her doctor. We wrote her a thank-you note and included money for our stay. In our time there, we saw the Tower of London, Buckingham Palace, and the changing of the guards. We went to Hyde Park and Kensington Gardens. We saw the National Gallery, the Tower Bridge, Big Ben. We shopped at Camden Market and Portobello Road Market. We walked around Piccadilly Circus in the West End. We visited the Houses of Parliament. We ate roast beef at Simpson's in the Strand in Covenant Gardens and we ate at an Indian Restaurant and drank at a local pub in the theatre district. We enjoyed our time there and saw a lot in the short time we were there.

Our next and final stop was Ireland. Chris had a relative, I think she was a great-aunt, who lived in an outer suburb of Dublin. Chris had contacted her asking if we could visit her when we were there. She was very hospitable and insisted that we stay with her. Each morning, she made us Irish breakfast tea with biscuits and homemade preserves. Then, we would take a local bus into Dublin and spend the day and evening there. We toured the National Botanical Gardens and Trinity College. We viewed the Book of Kells and the Old Library Exhibitions.

We visited the National Museum of Ireland and St. Patrick's Cathedral. We made a day trip and traveled to Blarney Castle and kissed the Blarney Stone—which in retrospect was very unhygienic! We walked through sections of Dublin every day and it was disheartening to us, taking the local bus home in the evenings, that we would pass many local pubs and see men and women staggering out of the pubs at a fairly early hour. We were visiting Ireland before the boom and life was difficult for many workers and even worse for the many people who were unable to find decent paying jobs. I think we saw more of the depressed scope of things because we were staying in a local neighborhood and not in a tourist area.

We saw as much as we could in the time we had and we had walked our way through most of it. It was a great experience and we came home exhausted but with no regrets. We were amicable traveling partners and we had the same goal—to see as much as we could in the time that we had. And it was a very good thing we were compatible, we shared a bed every night and sometimes, we were sharing a twin.

Chapter 4
Back to School

Once back home, I realized that I was at the place where I was thinking about major life changes and what I needed to do to make that happen. First and foremost was the issue of my short-lived marriage. Phil and I had different goals for what we wanted out of a marriage. After traveling and doing it on a modest scale, I was clear that a commune was not going to be in my future. I also was positive that I wanted a monogamous relationship or no relationship. More importantly, the free spirit orientation of my early twenties was being replaced with a perspective of more serious goals and behavior.

And after the heartbreak and disappointment of the separation, I had lost trust in Phil and was not inclined to put myself back in a place where I could get hurt yet a second time. I went home to visit my parents and we talked. I told them that I was probably going to move towards getting a divorce. My father, who was a local lawyer explained the New York no-fault divorce process. And we made a decision to have me use their home (where I had grown up) as my New York State residence, and my father would draw up the paperwork for a no-fault divorce based on irreconcilable differences.

Phil had begun a habit of dropping over the apartment, usually very late at night to plead with me to consider reuniting with him. Despite his vowing that things would be different, he didn't seem much different to me and coming around after midnight to plead had the opposite effect. My roommates and I were frustrated with his late-night disruptions. The next time he came around, I told him of my plan to go forward filing for divorce. Initially, he tried to talk me out of it, but I said I had made up my mind. I continued with my plans for the divorce and he was served with papers.

He made a few more attempts to dissuade me, at one point suggesting that we have a child to cement the relationship. Now that was one crazy idea considering the state of our relationship. He did sign the paperwork and return it to my father. My father submitted the paperwork to the Probate Court and a hearing date was set. I returned to my home and accompanied my father to Probate Court. The Judge read the paperwork, asked if this was really what I wanted and asked if there was any chance of reconciliation. After answering, "Yes" then "No" to both questions, he granted the divorce. The process took less than five minutes once we were before the judge. I was twenty-four years old, going on twenty-five, and I was divorced.

Returning to work, I continued to have serious qualms about whether this was the career I wanted. I had become the local shop steward for our Social Workers Union, which was affiliated with the AFL-CIO. In this position, I was able to volunteer to join committees on bettering the foster care system in our state and to better the workload, supervision, and education for Social Workers.

I served on a Union-Administration Joint Task Force to plan improvements to the Social Services Networks within the State. Despite all of these worthwhile endeavors, I felt that this was still a very unrewarding job. I grew tired of seeing vulnerable children taken out of their homes, moved in foster homes over and over, then returned home, only to often come back into care. It was just too depressing for me. One of my roommates, Mary, was a nurse in a big city hospital. She loved her work and was planning on furthering her expertise by returning to school to become a Nurse Practitioner for OB/GYN. Her enthusiasm inspired me to begin to think about making another major change in my life.

I applied to Boston College School of Nursing to a program called BA-BS transfers. It was geared to liberal arts majors who wanted a nursing degree, which was a science major. When I received my acceptance letter, I was informed that I was required to take a year of pre-requisites. I tendered my resignation to the Division of Child Guardianship and cashed out my retirement contribution, which I used to help fund Nursing School. I needed two semesters of anatomy and physiology, organic and inorganic chemistry, microbiology and a lab as well as a few other courses. After the prerequisites were successfully completed, the BA-BS transfers would be formally admitted into the Nursing degree program.

There were eight of us in total and we were kept as a group throughout the three years. We were a great group and as we were older than the other students in our program, we had the advantage of extreme focus. We weren't there to socialize, date, or to attend events—we went to class, studied, worked and led our lives based on our own particular life situation. Some of the members of our group were married and one of the women had a young son. Two of the eight of us were single men. One of the women was separated and I was divorced. The first year, I took classes three days a week, studied, and worked as a waitress about 30 hours a week.

Working as a waitress increased my stamina. I lied to get the job, stating I had previous waitress experience. My first three weeks there were tough. The waitresses were career waitresses and had worked at this large Jewish deli for years. Jack and Marian's was a famous restaurant in its heyday and a real moneymaker for these waitresses, who, for the most part, were single moms raising their kids. When I started there, the boom was over, the owner and his wife were having problems, and it was the beginning of its slide into oblivion.

Nevertheless, it could get really busy for brunch and lunch Wednesday through Sunday. The senior crew immediately spotted that I was a greenhorn in the waitressing business. One of the senior waitresses, Maria, was German-American and had much indirect power. She approached me and said, "I give you less than three weeks here, you'll never make it." She did nothing to assist me and would aggressively push past me or into me at the kitchen window. She would sometimes mix up my dishes, so that I would take a roast beef (rare) sandwich to a waiting customer to be berated as the roast beef was well done.

Things continued and I withstood her subtle and not-so-subtle harassment. When a month had passed and I hadn't quit, she did an amazing turn around. She approached me and said, "Since you surprised me and have stuck around, there's a few things you need to learn if you are going to survive here." She taught me how to stack filled lunch plates up my arm so that I could deliver food to my tables in one trip instead of three. She also taught me how to balance a tray full of drinks and how to unload them one at a time without tilting the balance of the tray, avoiding an upset.

She became my protector. She knew the regular customers and she knew which of them enjoyed being abusive to the wait staff. If I had one of these individuals at my table, I would find her standing at the end of my table as a customer started his usual routine and she would glower at him with her hands across her chest. One look at her and the customer would quickly change his stance. She taught me how to shuck strawberries so that I would be offered to stay during the slow times and get paid the minimum wage prepping the strawberries for the bakery, while the other wait staff was released with no pay for the next slow two to three hours.

I learned the culture of the place. I learned which kitchen chefs to avoid, which ones drank and their orders became unpredictable, and which chefs had the real power in the kitchen hierarchy. They had the real power in the restaurant and it was well worth your while to cozy up to them and let them know you appreciated what they did. If you were on the wrong side of the cooks, your dishes were the last to come out, or they did not signal you they were ready and you were likely to be bringing lukewarm food to the table instead of hot.

Another peculiar part of the culture was the systemized way the staff commandeered themselves to deal with the gypsies. A couple of times a year, a large group of gypsies would arrive and we would have to put several large tables together to accommodate them. The person whose station they were sitting in was considered the main waitress, but other waitresses assisted. The gypsies ordered many items each and once the food was served, a small army of waitresses positioned themselves around the outer perimeter of the tables. This was keeping watch as to who was getting up from the table and who still remained there.

This group of people excelled at somehow vanishing from the table without paying the bill. Their ability to do this in front of seasoned staff and the owners was uncanny. The first time they were assigned to my station, even with the help of a number of other waitresses keeping watch, they somehow exited and I was shafted with a large bill. The owner approached me and said, "Since this is your first experience with the gypsies, I won't hold you accountable, but the next time it happens, you will be responsible for the bill." This shook me since even he was keeping watch on my tables and he too was unable to prevent their dodging all of us. Also, what he was threatening me with was illegal. According to the law, I was not expected to pay. But, the reality was that if you wanted to keep the job, you followed the rules, legal or not.

I prided myself on successfully mastering this job and my tips and my schedule reflected it. But it was hard work. At the end of the day, all I wanted was a glass of wine and a basin of hot water with Epson salts in which to soak my feet. I worked at this busy deli for over eighteen months and husbanded my tips successfully. There were times my roommates, who were working full time at professional jobs, on occasion would ask to borrow money from me.

The last two years of nursing school were full time with classes and rotations to different hospitals for the clinical hands-on experience. Our schedule was at times gruesome. Some semesters, there were several days where we went to class from 9 to 2 and then had to drive at breakneck speed to a clinical rotation and hour away to arrive by 3 pm for a seven-hour shift. We would leave the rotation at 10 pm and drive an hour back home. Then we had treatment plans to develop and complete on the patient we had taken care of that day. The treatment plans had to be turned in the following morning. Sometimes, I was up until 4 am finishing the treatment plan, which included a full assessment, nursing diagnosis, the citing of relevant nursing theory, interventions and outcomes.

After collapsing into bed at 4 am, it felt tortuous to be awakened by my alarm at 5:30 am. I had 30 minutes to shower and put on a clean uniform, get my bag packed, and jump into the car pool at 6 am to drive an hour in an opposite direction for a different nursing clinical rotation. I would get home at 4 pm and have to do that rotation's treatment plan and then read assignments for classes or study for tests scheduled the next day. Our BA-BS transfer group developed our own study group for big tests like mid-terms and finals. We developed our own index card system for study and review. We had end of the year parties and although we were very different individuals, we were a closely bonded group. We all worked hard and we were all on the honor roll each semester.

Summers I worked as a nurse's aide for a few hospitals and I was hired for the night shift. I learned early on that this shift was not for me. It took a special kind of individual to work this shift and for some, it was the only way to have steady work and raise children. One summer job was I worked as a Nurse's Aide at a medical ward in a woman's hospital. There was a young woman on the floor who was dying. She had been diagnosed with ovarian cancer, which was inoperable. She was in her mid-twenties and had two young children at home. Her husband had brought her to Massachusetts for treatment, and he and the children lived in a state in the south. He would fly up to spend every other weekend with her. Their local church ran fundraisers to fund his air flights to Boston. When he was there, he slept in the bed with his wife and we gave them as much privacy as was possible in a hospital setting.

One summer night, I was asked to sit with her, as it had been reported by the day shift that she was not doing well. I was given the assignment to sit with her and take her vital signs every half hour. The nurse who supervised me told me that it would be OK for me to hold her hand while I was staying with her. I thought the assignment was odd. My usual assignment was to take the vital signs of all the patients twice during the night and to awaken the new post-operative patients and give them bed baths and massages from 5 to 6:30 am.

I went into the room and noticed that my patient looked very pale and appeared to be sleeping. I took her vital signs, which were extremely low and I told the supervising RN. She said not to worry, that the patient was not expected to live more than a week or two, and that there was a DNR (Do Not Resuscitate Order) in place. During the night, her vital signs continued to slow. At one point, she opened her eyes briefly and a few minutes later, I heard her sigh. I looked at her lying in the bed and observed that the blanket covering her was not moving up and down. I pressed the call button and the RN came to the room. I told her I thought the patient had expired. She looked at the clock in the room, and felt for a carotid pulse and confirmed that the patient had died.

I was upset and also angry. I felt everyone on the floor knew the patient was in her last hours and no one had really tried to prepare me. The nursing supervisor was called and she entered the room and asked me to help her prepare the body for the morgue. This procedure involved bathing the body and then wrapping it in linen gauze and then moving the body into a morgue bag for transportation to the morgue—a necessary but somewhat gruesome process. After some thought, and with some time, I decided that I had provided an important service being with this young mother in her final hours as a caring presence. But I continued to feel that the older nurses could have been more caring to me, a young nursing student just entering the field and someone who was the same age as the dying patient. (I was to learn in later years that my experience was not atypical. Sometimes, older more experienced nurses rather than mentoring a beginning nurse will instead make things more difficult.)

I would return home from working the night shift and find I was only able to sleep a few hours before the sunlight and the noise from the street below awakened me. This busy schedule left little time for dating and truth be told, dating wasn't high on my priority list.

Chapter 5
1975 – 1978: Mark

During the summer following my junior year at Boston College, one of my Stonehill college roommates, Doreen, invited me to a political party at the home of her brother. Her brother was sponsoring both Gerry Studds and Ted Kennedy for a Democratic Party fundraiser. Since I was a guest of my friend, I did not have to pay the ticket fee (which I never could have afforded). Her brother Patrick, who was sponsoring the event at his home, invited his good friend Marty and Marty's good friend Mark. (They didn't have to pay the ticket price either). After some mixing and walking around looking at the crowd, Doreen and I were introduced to Marty and Mark. We hit it off and began talking to them.

After a while, it became Mark and I talking, and we didn't notice that Doreen and Marty were no longer with us. We talked for several hours and there seemed to be a strong connection between us. I began to think to myself that I would like to see this man again. He was about 5'10, slim with a build that evidenced regular exercise; he had brown thick hair, blue eyes and he was handsome. He was also very personable and funny. It was so easy to talk with him and my somewhat 'introvert-ish' self was pleased at how easily he kept the conversation going. We had things in common, we both had liberal views; he had graduated from Boston College and I was now attending the same school. He and his friend Marty had a strong connection to the school and attended regularly the football and basketball games. He was working as an Accountant for a nursing home chain and I was attending school to become a nurse.

At the end of our time together as the party was wearing down, Mark asked for my phone number and asked if I would be interested in attending one of the Longwood tennis matches with him which were scheduled to open the following weekend. I said: "Sure, I'd love to go, but I know nothing about tennis so you will have to explain the basics when we get there." When we parted that evening, he said he would call me the following week. I slept at my friend Doreen's mother's home and drove back to Boston the following morning.

I continued my routine of classes, clinical rotations, and studying. By the following Wednesday, I began to anticipate a phone call from Mark. I had already told my roommates that I had met someone that I was interested in seeing. Friday came and went and no phone call came in for me. I began to doubt my perception that we had a connection between us. I was still hoping to hear from him, but I was expecting it to occur less and less. The following Friday, Mark called and said that the tennis championship matches had been postponed over a week due to the rainy weather.

He was expecting the matches to begin the following Monday and he was looking into procuring tickets for the following Friday evening. Then he asked if I was still interested in attending and I replied that indeed I was. We talked for several hours on the phone and he had an easy banter that made me laugh. In between light conversation, we interspersed information about ourselves and began the exploration of getting to know one another. Mark stated he would call the following week with an update on the matches.

I heard from him the following Thursday evening. He reported that the Friday matches had already been cancelled due to rain and his tickets had to be turned in and reassigned to another set of matches. Again, we talked for a few hours on the phone. For the second time in as many weeks, he said he would call me the following week with an update about the matches. I enjoyed the phone calls, but I was baffled as to the two-week postponement of our getting together based on the tennis matches. Although I was no tennis aficionado, I still did not understand that if the matches were rained out why couldn't we go to a movie or out to dinner? It was puzzling, but I wasn't writing him off yet. And I hadn't met anyone else in quite a while that had generated this degree of interest in me. That weekend, my roommates and I went to a local jazz club on

Saturday evening and listened to some good live music. It helped me be less preoccupied as to why I had not yet had a real date with Mark.

The following Wednesday evening, Mark called and this time, we were on for the tennis matches that Friday evening. After a long conversation, he related that he would pick me up at about 4:30 pm.

I was excited and glad that my Friday school schedule ended early and gave me some time to shower and get dressed in order to be ready by 4:30 pm. I had talked with Mary and Judy about what to wear to watch tennis matches and they weighed in on what would be the right type of casual attire. I was a little nervous as this was the first formal date I had been on in a while. I felt I was somewhat rusty and I knew nothing about tennis.

Mark arrived on time and as it was only 4:30, my roommates were not home and could not spy a look at him. The date was fun and Mark explained the basics of tennis and how points were scored so that I had at least a very basic understanding of what was going on. We watched at least two matches and as it grew dark, the spotlights came on. The stadiums were packed. I got home about eleven that evening and Mark said he would call the following week. Although we had watched quarter finals, it was unlikely that we would be attending more of the matches, as the semi-finals and finals matches were sold out in advance and also quite expensive.

Mark called again on Wednesday and that became the pattern going forward. This next planned date was going out to dinner with his roommate Billy, his friend Marty, and both of their dates. The plan was for Mark to pick me up at about 4 in the afternoon and to drive me out to his apartment in Waltham. The group would meet there, have drinks, and then go out to dinner. I met Billy, Mark's roommate and Mary, Billy's date. I also met Susanne, who was Marty's date. I liked them all and it was a fun group to be with. It was the start of many weekend group dates. We all got to know each other and became friends. We went to dinner, we watched BC football games live and on TV, and spent many weekends together for the next year.

Ironically, as a group, we were all somewhat in the same place—ready to fall in love and get serious about someone. We all met our mates at the right point in all of our lives. Our relationships were each moving at the same pace. We all had different circumstances that needed to be worked out, but we were moving as a group toward serious relationships, moving toward permanent commitments.

On a more intimidating scale was the prospect of meeting Mark's family. This occurred early in our relationship as the family had many parties following BC football games and for all the holiday occasions. I was really nervous about meeting Mark's family. I had met one of his younger brothers, Dennis and his wife, Marilyn early on. They were married with a young son and lived in an apartment. Mark introduced me to them first. Dennis jokingly referred to me as the 'gay divorcee'. That gave me a little hint that Mark's parents may not think I was suitable for their son.

I first met the rest of the family at a party after one of the football games. Marty and Susanne would also be going to Mark's Uncle Toss's home for the after-game party. It reassured me that I would at least have two people who I knew. And meeting the family, it was—not only Mark's brothers and sisters, but his two aunts, his uncle, cousins, and friends were all in attendance. Everyone was friendly and in good spirits. Conversation was casual and people were really enjoying themselves and it was clear that this was a frequent routine. I made through that first hurdle.

The second hurdle was Mark bringing me home to Sunday dinner at his parent's home. By now, I was aware that Mark was part of an Irish matriarchal family structure and that his mother's acceptance was of real importance. For this event, I was more nervous than I had been for the introduction at the family football party.

Mark's father, Jim, went out of his way to put me at ease and I loved him for it. He sensed I was nervous and talked to me in a gentle and funny way about this work and eased me into the conversation. Mark's mother was polite and friendly, but I sensed an initial appraisal was taking place. Mark's older brother, Jimmy, was also really friendly and tried to put me at ease. He was a natural storyteller and he regaled me with stories about his job as a high school science teacher and his part-time job as a football referee.

Mark's younger sister, Claire smiled at me a lot, but she was still in high school and quite shy. Mark's other sister, Lisa, was also welcoming but was in and out of the room, helping her mother with the dinner preparations. At some point in the afternoon, Mark's other younger brother Bernie arrived and I got to witness he and Jimmy entertain in mildly competitive fashion as they told one funny story after another. When Bernie realized that I was only part Irish but was also part Italian, he jokingly referred to me as 'Kathy Macaroni'. He meant it as a friendly gesture so I took no offence.

Watching the family dynamics, it was clear that Mimi, Mark's mother, was the lynch pin. And her opinion was taken seriously and with deference, even when it was clear that not everyone agreed with a particular opinion. As a family unit, they were not nearly as liberal as my family upbringing had been, so I was careful how much of my liberal views I shared. I learned not to comment when someone made a comment that I disagreed with. I did not want to make waves. I knew that if I was causing any serious tension, it would put Mark in a difficult position.

After dating over a year, Mark and I decided to get an apartment together in the same complex he resided in with his good friend Billy. I had brought Mark home to meet my parents and it was obvious that they liked him and saw him as a good fit with our family. I was glad that he had a strong work ethic and had goals for his future. He talked of eventually going back to school nights to obtain his MBA in accounting.

He and his friend Marty co-owned a condo in Wellfleet, Ma that they rented out during the summer and spent weekends there in the spring and fall. Mark talked of wanting to make enough money to be able to purchase a summer home on the Cape. He and a bunch of guys for the past number of years would chip in and rent a large home for a month or more every summer. He loved summers on the Cape and wanted time there as part of his future. I had spent time at two of these rentals on weekends in the summer as we were dating.

I liked that he kept himself fit and that he enjoyed running as a sport. He was very athletic—much more so than I. He ran, he played tennis and racquetball. I was very uncoordinated and couldn't tell five feet from fifty feet, putting me at a distinct disadvantage of mastering most sports. Mark liked to party and he was at his best socializing, actually working the room. I, on the other hand, entered any social situation looking for someone I knew and joined that person and felt no need to meet strangers. Making small conversation was always difficult for me, so I enjoyed watching Mark and seeing how easy and natural it was for him. He liked to dance after having a few drinks and so did I. His whole family knew many Irish ballads and they were a hallmark of parties they held where everyone joined in and sang. I found that I trusted him and it was easy to fall in love with him.

Once it was becoming clear that Mark and my relationship was getting serious and we were talking about marriage in our future, there was an obstacle to overcome. By now, I had regular contact with his family and saw them often on weekends. I was nearing the end of Nursing school and was looking into jobs at local hospitals. One job I was applying to was that of Psychiatric nurse at McLean Hospital in Belmont, Massachusetts. Mark and I had already talked about getting an apartment together in the same complex where he was currently living in Waltham. They were neighboring towns so my commute would not be difficult.

The issue Mark voiced to me was that his mother had said she would not be able to support any marriage between us unless it took place in a catholic church. He felt it was important for me to consider, but he would not walk away if I couldn't or wouldn't do it. I thought long and hard on that one. I didn't feel the need to marry Mark in a Catholic ceremony, I was already divorced, and my independent streak told me I should do what I wanted. The other side of me wanted to find a middle ground that was livable and I told myself I would explore what options were available.

Mark's family had very close friendships with a number of Jesuit priests, as Mark's Uncle, Alfred, was a Jesuit himself. They were also close with one diocesan priest Father Peter who was also a close family friend. I had already met three of these priests at family parties after BC football games. Mark talked with one of the Jesuits and they encouraged him to have me look into the catholic church annulment criteria and procedure, which would occur within the Bishop's Tribunal at the

Brighton campus. I obtained the information and the forms and read through the material. It involved a lengthy questionnaire of essays examining my prior marriage and the essence of my applying for an annulment centered around proving that based on Phil's and my mental state at the time of the marriage, that a genuine Catholic marriage had never taken place.

It was somewhat obscure, but it was a point in history when the Catholic Church was actually granting more annulments than at any time prior or in the future. I not only had to fill out the questionnaire and the application form, I also had to contact Phil and request that he agree to be interviewed when a hearing date was set. I also needed witnesses and my parents agreed to be interviewed as witnesses. Mark let his parents know that I was pursuing this avenue, and I knew that this was very important to them despite our not having had a direct discussion about it.

After being told that my application for annulment had been approved, there was a long wait. By this time, Mark and I had actually began making plans for a wedding around Memorial Day. And I grew increasingly anxious not having a hearing date as spring approached. We had already signed contracts with a caterer and obtained a hall for the reception.

At this point, I think the Jesuit friends of the family made some contact with the Boston Archdiocese Tribunal office. I finally received a letter with a hearing date for a time in mid-April. Whew! The day of the hearing, my parents had arrived and were staying in a local hotel. My friend Chris accompanied me to the hearing for moral support. We had bought a bottle of champagne, which was stocked in the trunk of the car along with plastic glasses. Mark was coming and would remain in his car in the parking lot of the archdiocese.

The hearing was a closed one and each person testifying was called in to be questioned by three priests on the Tribunal. Phil had arrived, and my parents and I greeted him pleasantly as we all waited in a hallway outside the hearing room. I was called in first and was asked several questions verifying the essays I had submitted in the application. After about ten minutes, I was dismissed. I can best describe the meeting as a legal religious court hearing. It was impossible to guess what any of the three tribunal judges were thinking. Their faces remained inscrutable. I was glad my part was over, but I had no idea how my responses were received.

Next, Phil was called to testify. He went in the room and about ten minutes later, he exited. He said he thought it went well and then he said his goodbyes to my parents and myself. When he received the notice of the annulment application, he had contacted me briefly and asked if this was what I wanted. When I told him that yes, it was important to me as I was remarrying and wanted to do so in the Catholic Church. He told me that he had met someone and was also planning to marry and that she was a journalist for a Rhode Island newspaper. I had wished him good luck. Now after saying goodbye to me in that hallway, he exited my life and another door had closed.

My father had a discussion with me a year prior about my divorce from Phil and how it had stirred up strong feelings within him about his Catholic beliefs. He said he had been worried about my future with Phil and was relieved when I made the decision to leave the marriage. He felt I deserved to have a life with a happy future and if the Catholic Church was going to penalize me for making a good decision for my future, then there was something wrong with the church rules. I know my mother felt the same way and it was clear that my father was strongly moved to have shared these thoughts with me.

My parents had been called in together and they were in the courtroom for a long time. Over thirty minutes passed while I waited in the hallway alone. When they finally appeared, they looked relaxed and said they felt it had gone well. A court clerk came out to inform us that the judges were conferring and that I would be called back into the courtroom when a decision had been made. My parents never shared with me their testimony, but my gut feeling was that it was the deciding factor. I think they felt responsible for a marriage that should not have taken place and that their beliefs they had grown up with about 'living in sin' overshadowed their scrutiny about whether this was a good match, did it have a chance of succeeding, and did it have the potential to make their daughter happy.

After about fifteen minutes, I was called back to the courtroom. The judges looked at me and one spoke up. I was told that I was being granted an annulment based on the fact that due to Phil's and my state of mind upon entering into a

Catholic marriage, no Catholic marriage commitment could have taken place. The fact that we had no children was also a mitigating factor in the decision. I was informed that their decision would be written up and sent to Rome. The decision would be presented to Pope John the 23rd and he would sign the annulment degree making it an official Catholic Church document. I thanked the judges and was escorted out to the hallway. The smile on my face was a dead giveaway as to the verdict and my parents hugged me. As we walked out to the parking lot smiling, Mark was popping the champagne bottle and Chris was filling the glasses. We toasted in the parking lot to our upcoming marriage.

About eight weeks later on May 28, 1977, Mark and I were married in a Catholic ceremony at St. Ignatius Church in Chestnut Hill, which was next to the BC campus. I had graduated from BC School of Nursing two weeks prior and our pinning ceremony also took place at St. Ignatius. It was Memorial Day weekend and was very hot and humid. The ceremony and Mass took place on Saturday early afternoon and the reception was held at a local hall in Brighton from 5 to 9 pm. It was a fun affair with friends and family including my BC 'BA-BS transfer buddies'. After the reception, Mark's parents hosted a large party back at their home. The house was filled with people and filtered out into the street. By midnight, I was exhausted and Marty drove Mark and I to a hotel near the airport for us to get a few hours of sleep before it was time to get to the airport for our flight the next morning to San Juan, Puerto Rico.

We flew to Puerto Rico and took a taxi to the condo on the water where we would be staying for most of our honeymoon. It was a gift of a benefactor of one of the Regan family's Jesuit friends. We arrived at the door to the condo and the key would not turn in the lock. After phone calls back home, someone was able to get in touch with our benefactor and he called the condo supervisor. He arrived at our door and confirmed that the key did not work in the lock. After conferring with the owner of the condo, a locksmith was called and a new lock and key was put in place. After two and a half hours, we were in our honeymoon suite.

Our stay there was romantic, fun, and restful. One weight that was in the background made our week less than perfect. Mark had been fired from his job one week before the wedding. He had called me from the apartment the evening that it had occurred. He was very upset and he had been blindsided. From what he told me, his boss called him into the office and related that the company was being bought out by another, larger nursing home chain. When they audited the books, they found some *irregularities*.

Apparently, the VP of finance was suspected and he was terminated. Mark's boss would be taking that position. He said that he knew Mark had nothing to do with the fixing of the books, but he needed to look like he was cleaning house so he was letting Mark go. We decided to go ahead with the wedding date and not to discuss what had occurred. There was an elephant in the room with us at times. When the honeymoon was over, Mark needed to find work.

While on our vacation, we took a flight to the island of Saint Thomas and stayed at the Pineapple Inn Resort. We loved Saint Thomas. It was quiet, beautiful, and the temperature was perfect for spending time out of doors. Meals were served on the veranda with birds flying in and out. There was always a breeze and there was no humidity. The island was beautiful and the people were friendly and welcoming.

One morning at breakfast, we looked over and spied a man and his wife. On closer observation, it was 'Ted', the actor from the Mary Tyler Moore show. Mark got such a kick of seeing him that for the remainder of our stay there, he did imitations daily of 'Ted' saying "Good Morning, Mary" in Ted's TV voice.

The week went quickly and before we knew it, we were back in the Boston area in our Waltham apartment with me starting a new job and Mark looking for work.

Chapter 6
1978 – 1980: Work and Home

My first job out of nursing school proved more than challenging. I was a nurse on the 'Orange Unit, Hall Mercer'. This was a locked child psychiatric unit at McLean Hospital. It was a Harvard teaching hospital so the unit was run by Harvard psychiatry residents. It was a very traditional model of psychiatric care for children. One unsettling observation I made while there, was realizing that a child would be diagnosed and thought of as being very sick until the insurance money either ran out or the insurance company balked at the long stay, then suddenly the plan was to discharge the patient home. This was before the days of managed care so hospital stays were much longer then.

The building in which the child units were housed had won architectural awards. It was a nightmare. It was a poured concrete modern structure that had a sunken day hall. Kids and visitors were falling and tripping in that room with concrete sunken seats. The halls on the units were circular around the perimeter of the nurse's station and all the bedrooms were off these hallways. The halls having floor to ceiling concrete walls meant there was no line of vision in the hallway from the nurse's station.

I hadn't been on the unit three months when I was carrying a check's board, doing checks. Doing checks was a task on all psychiatric units. The person doing checks is responsible for locating and documenting where each patient was at a given point in time. Different patients had different 'privileges'. Some children might be on five-minute checks and another might be on 15-minute checks. The staff person assigned to do checks was to do so for an hour at a time and was expected to do no other task other than walk up and down the unit locating each child and noting where they were. It is an important and serious task of making sure everyone is safe on the unit at each point in time.

And when adverse things happen such as an assault, self-abusive behavior, suicide attempt, an escape or a patient making allegations against another patient or against a staff person, the check sheet is an important document regarding liability. I was doing checks and entered a two-bed boys' room to document the patients in the room. As it was room time, I expected to see the room's two male patients sitting on their respective beds. When I entered the room, and found both beds unoccupied, I turned and began to exit the room.

Both boys had climbed on the top of their closets and as I approached the door, they both jumped off the top of the closets and knocked me to the floor. I called for staff, but the nurse in the nurse's station couldn't hear me. The boys were on top of me and pinning me to the floor. Another child in the next room heard my yell for staff and he came running. I asked him to go to the nurse's station to get staff which he did. Staff came running, and I was released from the grips of the two children. The two boys were led to the Quiet Room and were secluded, meaning the doors were locked. This was done as a consequence for having assaulted me.

The units, in that building, all had numerous blind spots, which is a disaster for any psychiatric unit. It led to the temptation for dysregulated children to act out rather than relax. Riots were a routine in this building; the administration was not good and morale was terrible. Sickout calls were routine, which meant that safe staffing levels became an ongoing issue. The alarms for rioting were so common that staff from the adult units refused to float to the children's building to fill the sick calls. I worked one evening shift and was told I was expected to cover two units by myself! I could not believe my supervisor would suggest such a thing. I was covering two units that were not in close proximity and I was taking on the role of four nurses. Each unit had two nurses on the day and evening shifts. One nurse was in charge and the other nurse did the medications for all patients on the unit.

The supervisor said she would check on me regularly and to call if there was a problem. When I did my initial check on the other unit I was covering, I learned that they had also had a sick call from a mental health worker so they were down two nurses and a mental health worker. My unit was down one nurse.

I had a sick feeling in my stomach that this was a set up for disaster. When we brought the children to the dining hall for their early dinner, I could see that the children from the other unit had a group of 10 and 11-year-old boys who seemed revved. They started throwing butter pats at the ceiling with the goal of hitting the fire alarms and setting off the alarms. When the staff of that unit escorted them back to the unit, they asked me to accompany them to give out some PRN meds to the children who appeared the most agitated. There were about four boys who appeared to be becoming increasingly angry and they were escalating one another. I gave out the needed meds and returned to my unit. The children on my unit seemed on edge and the staff suggested they go to their rooms for 30 minutes and then everyone would watch a movie.

Shortly after this, the announcement came over the building PA system calling for staff on the unit I had left with a Code Red, (meaning assault). I went to that unit and found kids running around while three mental health workers were trying to hold two children down on the floor as they tried to punch and hit the staff. I called hospital security and notified them we had a Code Red and that we needed their help. No sooner had I done that, when heard another building announcement that there was a Code Red on my unit.

I called back the hospital security force and said to send even more help. Children were running wild and throwing things on both units and there just was not enough staff to contain the situation. The more timid children were crying and the staff on my unit was trying to keep the scared children in the day hall with one staff while the other two staff were chasing down the other kids. It was a horrible situation.

Security officers arrived and assessed the situation. Word had spread on the remaining two child units in the building and children were now agitated and acting out on those units also. This is every staff person's nightmare, the contagion effect. The units were collapsing under the domino effect as more children escalated. Security called the main hospital and asked for any male staff on the numerous adult units to be freed up to assist us in regaining order in the building. More help arrived and we had already filled all four quiet rooms in our building. Security and male staff from the main buildings using four security cars made two trips to board eight children from our units on the adult units temporarily.

My supervisor arrived finally and stated she wanted to meet with me immediately. I told her that was not possible as I was needed to give out medications on both units I was covering. She said she would wait for me to finish. We met in the tiny medication room on my unit. She began by saying she wanted me to draw a diagram of where every staff person was at the time of the riot. I could not believe it. The staff, the children, and I had just gone through a very traumatic experience and her response was not to apologize and try to comfort us or to apologize for placing us in this unsafe position.

She wanted a diagram so she could point out what I had done wrong in not being able to thwart the rebellion. Normally, I believed that for me to succeed in any job, I needed to be respectful of my boss. I was so upset and angry that I actually got into a huge screaming match with her and told her that her lack of support and understanding was the last thing I had expected in this crisis. I told her that I would get her diagram and the report of the night's events to her when I could, but I could not spend another minute talking with her.

I slammed out of the medication room and went to the Nurse's station. She came out of the med room five minutes later and left the unit. The staff reported that everyone had heard our shouting match through the door and that they were glad I had said the things I had. I spent several hours, after my shift was over, drawing her the diagram of both units as best I could after I interviewed the staff on both units. My report drew strong conclusions that the staffing levels that evening were totaly insufficient and were a set up for disaster.

The next day at Clinical Rounds, the staff present agreed that there was insufficient staff to have run both units. The psychiatric resident took steps to discharge patients who could go home and to stop admissions for several days to give the units in the building a time to recoup. I knew my time here was limited. Although McLean Hospital was viewed as one of the top psychiatric facilities in the country, I was not impressed with the care given to the children and their families. I had lost total respect for my nursing supervisor and I felt she was incompetent for her position. Our relationship was distant and cool, and I avoided supervision sessions with her whenever it was possible to do so. She apparently felt the same way as she cancelled supervision sessions herself for one reason or another. I relied on the more senior nurses on the unit for advice and felt their approach was level-headed.

I started looking for another job the day after the riots. I had applied for a position as an administrator for a Home Health Care Agency that was a start-up. I was offered the position, but I asked for a week's time to give my decision. It was a way out of my current position, but it held no spark for me. I just couldn't get excited about it. I had also applied for a position as a psychiatric nurse for a Day Treatment Center in a community mental health center in a city south of Boston, but I got no response to my application.

I was somewhat puzzled. I did call the mental health center and they related that they had received my application but offered no additional information. I thought that they were probably not interested in me and maybe they thought I was not a good fit with their agency. The job was working with chronic adult psychiatric patients in the community and my experience had been of working with children in the hospital. I had given up hearing from them and was again scouring the want-ads for other jobs that might be of interest.

Then some three weeks later, I received a call from the Program Director of the Day Treatment Center to come in for an interview. I was told it would be a group interview. I had no experience with group interviews, so I did not know what to expect. I arrived at 9 am and waited in a chair in the hallway for thirty minutes. The interview took place in a church basement, which was where the program was located. Adult clients walked back and forth passing me in the hallway. Some even said hello. Finally, the door opened and I was asked by one of the staff to come into the room.

The interview was nothing like anything I could have imagined. I was asked numerous questions about how I would handle different situations that might occur with patients attending the program. I was asked what activities I liked or what talents I possessed and how could I incorporate them into ideas for the program. I was asked if I was a self-starter, that staff were expected to be creative and come with ways to better the program and be able to implement their ideas. It was a very challenging interview and although the questions related to job at hand, I got this feeling that people were hostile and I could not figure out what I was doing or saying to generate this hostility. One staff member, Bernice, who had been introduced as a nurse gave me smiles of encouragement. Finally, I was asked to leave the room while they conferenced on what I had said. I went back to my seat in the hallway and prepared myself to be told that I was not what they were looking for.

When I was called back in, the Director of the Program, Ellen, spoke about the group's reservations despite my answers, which they had liked. She went on to say that they were very upset that I seemed to think that they could be pressured by politicians to give me a job and that they could never be influenced by such pressure. I was totally perplexed and my face must have displayed my puzzlement. I had no idea to what she was referring. I asked her what she meant by her comments. Ellen went on to tell me that they had received a call from a Massachusetts representative's office and the aide was requesting that I be considered for the position. I responded that I did not even know who this representative was, nor did I know if he was in my district, nor did I know anything about Massachusetts politics.

I had gone to school in Massachusetts and had gotten a job here, but I had no involvement with any politician. They were able to tell that I was stymied. Ellen then asked me: "Do you know anyone who would know this politician?" I thought of Mark, but I didn't think he would contact a politician without mentioning it to me or asking if it was alright.

I told Ellen: "I have a husband, but I don't think he would do this without asking me." I offered to call him. I was able to contact Mark and he said he had not done anything, but he did remember telling his friend, Peter, who was politically connected, that I had applied for this job and hadn't heard back from them. He said he did not ask Peter to contact anyone, but he bet Peter had gone ahead and done this, thinking it might help me.

I went back into the office and reported what I had learned from Mark. I again assured them that I had nothing to do with the politician and apologized for Mark's friend's behavior. They must have believed me as I was asked to stay for lunch. It was a community lunch that was held every Wednesday. It was a time when the staff ate lunch with the clients of the program. I was placed at a seat along a long four-sided table and put between two clients of the program. It was a test to see how I would interact as one of the patients was considered challenging. She asked me many personal questions and I gave her brief responses that did not share too much personal information.

She, on the other hand, gave me way too much personal information about herself. I finally realized that my tactic needed to be one of distraction. So, I began to pepper her with questions about the program, what she liked and disliked, what groups she attended, how long she had been coming to the program, etc. Periodically, I would look up and around the long table and observe the staff discretely checking me out. The patient on my other side was quiet and I tried to draw him out a bit. He was only able to give me one-word answers, but I could see that he was glad to have been given some attention.

After lunch, the staff started the afternoon groups and I was given a copy of their current schedule. I met with Ellen, and she said that they would like to offer me the job. There was one more step. I had to meet with a Psychiatric Nurse at the main Mental Health Center and she had to approve my being hired. At that time, the Day Treatment Center was only open three days a week. So two days a week, I would need to work in the Psychiatric clinic at the Mental Health Center seeing patients and helping in a Prolixin Clinic and here I would be supervised by the Psychiatric Nurse, Pauline. I met with her and we hit it off easily. She was friendly and open and stated she would call Ellen and tell her the interview went well.

As soon as I got the call from Ellen that I had been approved for the position by the Mental Health agency, I told her I would be able to start in two weeks. I was happy to be starting a new job with a new focus and so glad to be leaving

Hall Mercer. I typed up my letter of resignation that evening. I went to work the following afternoon. I contacted my supervisor and told her I needed to meet with her. She came over during my shift and I presented her with the letter of resignation. She was less than gracious and said my leaving this way was extremely unprofessional.

She related that for a professional job, the required notice was at a minimum three weeks and four weeks were preferred. I told her that was not possible as I would begin work at my new job in two weeks' time. I was ready to jump for joy that I would no longer have to endure meetings with her. I was glad that I didn't share with her what I had been thinking when she was talking to me. What I had wanted to say was: "You should be glad I'm not walking out the door right now. I can't even imagine having a worse supervisor!"

My new job was great! My boss Ellen was fantastic! She was short in stature, but her presence was as big as life itself. She was a zany, creative, bright, big idea person with a sharp social conscience. She had the conviction, the energy, and the resources to make things happen. Her expectations were clear: find out what the program needs, come up with ideas as to how to improve things, then go off and do them. She was the antithesis of a micromanager. I was expected to be independent, creative, and productive. How I did that was on me. The same was true to a lesser degree to the other staff. I was at this job for almost four years and it was a wonderful experience. I grew as a psych nurse, but in addition, I grew as an administrator, learning how to keep several balls in the air at the same time.

I ran groups, some co-lead, some solo, I ran the medication clinic at the day treatment center with a fantastic psychiatrist, Leo. The clients all called him 'Dr. Leo'. He was approachable and kind, smart and willing to think outside the box. He respected my expertise and judgment. We were a good pair seeing to the medication needs of the clients at the center. I became the Assistant Director, under Ellen. The day-to-day running of the program was my domain as well as developing the program schedule of groups and assigning the staff to the groups. This was done four times a year and developing the group schedule was a major task. I was also in charge of intakes of new clients and developing an individualized schedule for each new admission to the program. We also expanded to a five-day program and we doubled the daily census.

A few months after I started work, I learned I was pregnant. I was excited and so was Mark. He had found a job within a couple of months after we married. At this time, he was working for Raytheon as an auditor. This meant he would be traveling whenever the audit to which he was assigned was, for a Raytheon subsidiary that was out of state. Usually, these trips lasted two weeks, sometimes three. Life was good.

We had jobs we liked, I was pregnant, and we bought a starter home. During this time, Boston was still in the throes of the desegregation debacle. As a result, home prices plummeted. This worked to our advantage. We were interested in finding a home in West Roxbury, which was considered a desirable Boston suburb. We were able to purchase three-bedroom, one-and-half bathroom brick home on a quiet street in West Roxbury for $39,000! And we only needed $5,000 down payment for a mortgage. My pregnancy was going smoothly and I finally shared the news with my boss and coworker. I had planned to resign the end of May and was due to deliver at that time. We placed an ad for a psychiatric nurse to fill my position. I was involved in the interview process and after my replacement was hired, I was there to orient her before I left.

I passed my due date and after two weeks, the doctor gave a date for me to be induced. I went to my last appointment, which now was 42 weeks and the doctor put the stethoscope on my abdomen and listened and tried again several times. He finally looked up and said: "I can find no heartbeat."

I was in shock and dazed. I said: "I don't understand. What does that mean?"

He said in response: "Your baby has died." He said he wanted me to be hospitalized immediately and to be induced that day. I called Mark and told him I was on the way to the hospital and for him to meet me at Beth Israel Hospital. I have no idea how I managed to get to the hospital and I amazed to this day that the doctor gave me this horrific news and sent me out to drive alone to be admitted to the hospital.

The next few weeks were devastating for me. When I arrived at the hospital, I was put in a labor room and was induced with a seaweed agent that was intended to speed up my hours in labor. But it was so strong that it greatly intensified the contractions so the experience was horrific. When delivery was immanent, I was wheeled into the delivery room. I delivered the baby and there was dead silence in the room. No one spoke. (For the next ten years, I had flashbacks and nightmares reliving that devastating silence.)

The doctor finally spoke and strongly advised that I not view my baby. He stated that the baby had not been alive for some time and did not look like what a normal newborn would look like. I named her Allison on the death certificate. She was given time of death as the time of delivery on that June 14th. We had a funeral ceremony and burial at a local cemetery and one of the Regan family Jesuit priests presided over the ceremony. A local funeral director donated to the hospital funeral arrangements and burial for parents who had lost a baby.

When Ellen had heard the news, she arrived at the hospital the day after I delivered before I was due to be discharged. She informed me that she had found a way to fund a position for me and that I had a job. She encouraged me to take two weeks to rest before returning to work. She also suggested I see a therapist to help Mark and I deal with what had occurred. I took her suggestion and we saw the psychiatrist she had recommended.

He asked a lot of questions and came to the conclusion that we were talking about what had happened, we were sharing our feelings of loss with one another, and I was suffering from 'uncomplicated grief'. I just had go through it and come out the other side. He said he was available if I thought I needed it at some future point. It was rough for a while. I was glad to go to work and take my mind off my grief for eight hours a day, but I usually cried myself to work and back in my car. Mark was allowed to do local audits for the first six weeks, but then he was on the road again. I would find myself pacing around the house sometimes for hours.

I threw myself back into work and was glad that it consumed a lot of my energy. This was the '70s and it was the heyday of deinstitutionalization in Massachusetts. I served on a Task Force with a psychologist in our program, Marty, and some officials from the regional office of the Department of

Mental Health. We were encouraged to write grants to aid in the deinstitutionalization efforts within our county to bring patients from Medfield State Hospital back to the community. We wrote a grant and it was approved. The initial phase was to move eight men and eight women from the wards of the state hospital into apartments we would rent and manage in our community. It was an exciting endeavor but also a challenging one.

We went out to the state hospital to get input from the staff caring for the patients. They were very resistive and sometimes outright hostile to us. Some of the staff had worked at the local state hospital for generations. It was a major industry for this small bedroom town 25 miles from our day treatment center, which was located in Quincy, a city 15 miles south of Boston. It became clear that we would have to depend on the hospital medical records in determining who might be appropriate to move out to the community. The staff was not helpful and on one occasion, a nurse locked us out on a porch with the patients and did not come back for over an hour.

The patients had no desire to leave the hospital. Some had been there for over 20 years and it was the only home they remembered. Some patients had privileges called 'unlimited on-grounds'. This meant that they could wander on the large campus from after breakfast until dinner time. They were left to themselves and the thought of being in a city and having all sorts of people around was terrifying to them. Some of the patients worked in sheltered workshops where they felt productive but were under no stress. Any change in this routine was considered unfavorable.

After a lot of discussion and planning, the Department of Mental Health (DMH) decided that in order to build in a slow gradual transition, there would be a slow phase-out of the hospital workshop program. And there would be a bus trip every Wednesday from the hospital to our Day Treatment Center for a busload of patients and some of the hospital staff. The Department of Mental Health (DMH) also allayed the fears of the hospital staff stating that in the initial phases of deinstitutionalization, all staff would be maintained by transfer to other units. Then, in later phases, jobs would be created within the DMH and within the community as options for hospital staff down the road.

When the bus trips started, our client attendance on Wednesday doubled. Some Wednesdays, there would be 20 or more extra patients joining us. A typical day started with the clients having coffee in the day hall. Regular clients already had a schedule of groups they attended on any given day. The State Hospital clients were added into the Current Events Group, the Crafts Group, and the Art Therapy group. We served a big lunch every Wednesday led by Janice, one of our staff and a group of clients who had a desire to learn how to prepare a meal. Staff joined this big meal and sat interspersed among the clients.

Over time, we began to identify potential clients for our first set of apartments. We started out with five women and five men in our initial group. We began to have meetings with them to discuss what life would be like in returning to the community. They were terrified. We developed special groups just for this group. One of our mental health workers, Tom, was wonderful with all our clients, but he was particularly gifted in his acceptance of this group and their fears. His calm, accepting demeanor, and presence alone decreased their anxiety. He took them on local buses, teaching them how to use the local buses and manage tokens.

He taught them basic money management. My friend Debbie (who had been hired as my replacement) and I taught basic cooking classes. It was not gourmet cooking by any means and most recipes involved some type of Campbell's Cream of Something soup. One of the men in our group, Tom, had some cognitive deficits and also difficulty retaining information. It became a weekly ritual in our cooking group for Tom to say, "But Debbie, I just don't understand the difference from a stove and an oven. Can you go over it again?"

Marty and I ran a 'Regulations Group'. We wanted the clients to feel comfortable in their move to the community. So we felt for them to have buy in for living in the community; they needed to have a say in what their daily life would entail. We were so surprised by the number of rules they wanted built into the program in order to feel comfortable.

Some examples of rules that they voted on unanimously:

1. Parents can only visit once a week and only come to dinner once a month. (Some of these clients were already in their fifties!)
2. No sleepovers.
3. Medication for each roommate must be in a locked box.
4. No loud music or yelling.
5. Each roommate was expected to take their medication as prescribed.
6. No alcohol.
7. If a roommate stops taking their medication, the other residents will report this to the staff.

They all agreed that they wanted things highly structured.

Getting the apartments ready became a group project. We bought all the furniture from Unfinished Furniture and brought them to the Day Treatment Center. John, our maintenance man was a fantastic handyman and he assembled the beds, bureaus, end tables, coffee tables, etc. Then we put tarps on the floor and the staff and volunteer clients sanded all the furniture, and then stained and varnished each piece. It was a labor of love. The staff set up the apartments with the furniture, lamps, linens, pictures, and even stocked the kitchen with staples.

As we had expected, we would lose a few patients who just were not ready for this transition. We had four women ready to move in and we had four men for the initial two apartments. After the move in, we held house meetings weekly for the first six months and then every other week. We later opened another female and another male apartment. The third phase involved a group residence for more severely impaired individuals who would need staff supervising their residence. This was called the 'BIP House', otherwise known as the Behavioral Intensive Program. This endeavor required community approval and we attended community meetings to allay the neighbors' fears and to counter the 'NIMBY' (Not In My Backyard) bias.

Things weren't always easy at the center. Clients sometimes went off their meds and decompensated and would need to be re-hospitalized. We would have to do the evaluation, have Dr. Leo sign the pink paper (which was the legal document called a Section 12, requiring the need for hospitalization), call for an ambulance, and have the patient sent back to the local psychiatric hospital. I remember one Thanksgiving dinner at the center, which was held the week before Thanksgiving on a Wednesday. We had a big crowd and had set up extra tables. David, a client I saw for medication appointments had not shown up in several weeks. The rumor mill from other clients who had seen him said he was off his meds and did not look good. He was very paranoid when off his meds but was quiet and gentle when he was taking them.

He showed up for the meal and would not sit down. He kept pacing around the room. The next report I received was from Janice, who was supervising the cooking of the meal. She came to me upset and said that someone had left open the sharp drawer (where all sharp items including knives are kept). And David had grabbed a large carving knife and was pacing with it. The clients were very edgy and worried. I told another staff person to call the police and I went into the day hall.

I just kept saying in a quiet voice, "David, you do not want to hurt anyone, just give me the knife." I kept my voice calm and repeated this mantra over and over again. Then I asked him: "David, look at me. I know you and you would never do this unless you were upset. Let me help you, but you need to give me the knife first". Finally, I saw that his eyes recognized me and the glazed look had faded for a minute. In that instant, I put out my hand and he handed me the knife. He continued to pace and the police arrived. He went with them without putting up a fight. But that had been a tense 10 minutes.

After my promotion to the position of Associate Director, I found I liked managing the program and all its varied components. Our schedule changed four times a year. I would send out a memo asking the staff to send me back a list of the groups that they wanted to run and their preferences for the day and time of the group. I would take everyone's submissions and then work on the schedule. I had huge sheets of poster papers that were lined. I would make five columns for each day of the week on a horizontal plane and then write the hours of each day in a vertical plane. Then I took all papers with the staff's submissions and tried to fill them in the appropriate boxes. This was a huge undertaking; some hours, we had three groups running at one time. Other days, I had to block out time for the medication clinic.

I was also responsible for the admissions to the program, so I had to free up myself for two hours on two days to do admissions. It was a challenge; it was like solving a big puzzle and I was proud of my accomplishment every time we rolled out a new schedule. Debbie became my good friend and we maintained that friendship over the years. Ellen was my mentor and she brought out the best in me. I am forever grateful for her tutelage and her faith in me. She also became a life-long friend.

Chapter 7
On the Home Front

We were trying to start a family and were having some difficulty. I would get pregnant and Mark would be excited and bring me flowers. Then I would miscarry and be so disappointed. If Mark had understood me better, he would have known that receiving flowers would have meant so much more if they were bestowed on me to help me with the disappointment of losing another pregnancy. Child bearing seemed so difficult and so fraught with disappointment.

What should have been a happy task for me generated sadness and angst. I began to talk about the idea of adoption. I felt I couldn't keep going through the motions of trying to get pregnant. I felt raw and I wanted a live baby in the house before I tried again. I was still in a place that when people talked of baby showers or of people they knew having babies, I would discretely leave the room. And it seemed that everywhere I turned, there was talk of babies.

I began to explore various adoption agencies. I initially explored Catholic Charities and found out that I did not qualify for their program. I needed a letter from a physician stating I was not able to conceive. That was not my problem. I became pregnant easily enough, my problem was carrying a baby to term. I looked into several other agencies and we settled on the Alliance for Children. It was initially located in Wellesley, Ma. I sent for information and received a brochure. They had an information meeting in the evening once a month. Mark and I attended and the staff was welcoming. They served coffee and cookies and had books displayed of children they had placed in families over the years.

The Program Director, Phyllis, was the first to speak to the group and she gave a history of the founding of the program and its growth to the present time. Next two of the Social Workers introduced all the staff of the program. Then they took turns describing the various countries that they had alliances with: India, El Salvador, Columbia, Mexico, Russia, Romania, China, Korea, etc. They described how each program differed based on the agreements and rules set by the host country. And the cost varied greatly based on the country. At that time, Mexico was the most expensive country they dealt with; charging $7,000.00! Back then, that was a lot of money and it was money we did not have. The price was also influenced by politics. The US and Mexico had strained relations at that point in time and there was a little of the 'let's stick it to the Gringos' in that high price.

They were placing most of their babies with Swedish couples. (The Swedish government subsidized all adoptions.) India had the lowest cost at that time, as they had more girls in orphanages than they could care for. An obstacle here was that we were ineligible for this program. It was run by Mother Teresa and her program stipulated that no parent could have been divorced. Even though the Catholic Church had granted me an annulment, I was still ineligible! As the meeting broke up, we were encouraged to look at the pictures of children who were currently available. It was to get ideas about what our interests were and what we could imagine in making a family. There was a second information meeting for those who attended and who wanted more information. We attended this second meeting a few weeks later.

During that time, Mark and I discussed what we thought we could handle and what was more than we felt we could reasonably undertake. We wanted a child that was fairly young, about two or younger. We felt we did not have the skill set to take on a child with physical or cognitive challenges.

The second meeting talked about the process itself, the home study and what it entailed, the costs of various programs and the anticipated wait once the home study process was completed and approved. They also talked about the option of couples paying for their home study and the fees for the various programs' fees by credit cards such as American Express. It seemed a little weird. But this was a group of people trying very hard to make families.

We told the staff that night that we were, in fact, wanting to proceed and that we were interested in a young child from Columbia. About a week or two later, we received a phone call from Judy, the social worker who had been assigned to complete the home study. She set up an appointment to meet with us at our home. She inspected our home and then sat and explained in more detail the home study process, the wait, placement, and then follow-up by the agency. She projected that it would take up to three months to complete the actual home study. She left us with a packet of essay questions that would be incorporated in the home study document they developed. Once she received the completed essays, she would go over them and then set up another appointment.

It asked questions about our childhoods and how we were raised. What were our thoughts on discipline, our thoughts about having a blended family, and how to incorporate the different cultures within our family. Mark and I discussed each question and then I would type out our responses. It took about three weeks to complete the essays. I mailed them back to Judy at the Alliance. After another week had gone by, she called to set up another appointment. She met with Mark and me, and asked follow-up questions on some of our answers and other questions about our finances, my plans for adoption leave and she gave us her suggestions.

We also had to sign permission for the agency to do background checks on us that were sent to the FBI office. She told us that once we were approved, we needed to be fingerprinted at the state police office and that we needed passports obtained. The passport pictures would accompany our home study when it was sent to Columbia. I would also need to go to the Columbian Embassy in Copley Square to obtain stamps and permits needed for the Columbian Government to allow a Columbian child to be sent out of the country for adoption.

I was very anxious about the background check and didn't know if my being at protest marches and rallies would show up and undermine the adoption process. I never mentioned it in the adoption home study, but I knew that the FBI or local law enforcement had photographed everyone present at some of the more well-known anti-war rallies in New Haven, Boston, and

Washington, DC. I had prayed that it was now such old news that any photos taken were in a storage box somewhere or destroyed.

Finally, after months, we got the word. We had been approved by the Alliance For Children for adoption and our paperwork had been sent to Medellin, Columbia. Now we started the wait. We waited and waited. In Columbia, adoptions were done on a regional level. The Judge presiding in a particular region gave the consent and signed the adoption release. Our application was sent to an Alliance representative in the Medellin region of the country.

The court official from the Judge's office in Medellin called the Alliance every couple of weeks to ask: "How are the Regan's doing? It won't be long now!" As time dragged on, the agency no longer updated us on the calls from Columbia. As other couples received their children from other places within Columbia and we remained at the top of the list for Medellin, but nothing happened, the agency called us. They asked if they could put us on other lists for a young child. We said yes.

I was at work. Everyone at work knew I was waiting for the most important phone call of my life and at this point, no one answering the phone was going to take a message if it was for me. I was asked to come to the front desk. I picked up the phone and it was Judy. She asked if I was sitting down—I was. She said that she had received a call from adoption agency in Texas. They sometimes worked with it when that agency in Texas had a baby they were having difficulty placing. She said that we had a son, who was Mexican-American and he was fourteen weeks old. He was in good health and had spent the first fourteen weeks of his life in a convent being cared for by one of the nun's there.

His mother had released him at birth, but the biological father (who was married and had children of his own) appealed to the court to gain custody. The judge gave the father 14 weeks to come up with a viable plan to care for the child. The deadline had occurred the day before and the father did not appear in court. The judge granted the final release at the end of business that day. I was told that our son was seven pounds at birth and 21 inches long. Judy said she would get back to me with more details, but we should expect to receive our son in a week's time.

I got off the phone and was speechless with tears running down my cheeks. Ellen sent someone out to the liquor store and had them purchase a cartload of champagne. It was the end of the day, and as the clients left, Ellen and the staff decorated the day hall for a celebration. I called Mark at his work and told him everything I could remember. I told him to come join us in the celebration. It was a great party and I was so jazzed up that no matter how many drinks I had, I was stone-cold sober.

Chapter 8
1980 – 1986: Our Family Begins

The day had finally arrived! It was the first week of November, 1980. We were so excited that we were unable to contain our excitement. Fifteen long months of waiting, a period that seemed endless, and now just minutes away and we would become parents. Our joy was contagious. Somehow, the news had spread among the throng of people waiting at the terminal gate that we were waiting for our baby son to arrive from Texas. Mark and I were excited but also very nervous. It was hard to concentrate.

My mom and dad had driven from New York to be with us at Logan Airport, in Boston. Mark's mom and dad were also there. My good friend Debbie and her husband Mike came with cameras to record the event. We were a boisterous group and the focus of attention in the waiting area. The airport was our delivery room. For a few minutes, Mark and I were distracted as Judy, our social worker from adoption agency, came over with packets of papers for us to sign. It was now official. All systems were to go.

The loudspeaker announced the arrival of the American Airlines flight from Amarillo, Texas at our gate. Suddenly, it became very quiet. People started filtering out of the arrival gate and walking into our waiting area as they made their way through the terminal. They all knew what was happening. Their eyes searched the crowd, fixed on our group, and started smiling at us. Some even lingered, wanting to be part of the event. Oh God! What a feeling.

A young woman approached our group carrying a bundle in her arms wrapped in a light blue blanket. The next few minutes were confusing. I was smiling so hard that my jaw hurt. I was so overcome with emotion that I was almost unable to move. I, who would cry during a Hallmark commercial, could not shed a tear. The woman walked up to me and handed me my son. She said: "You have a beautiful son. I wish you much happiness," and with that, she placed him in my arms. Everyone was crying, strangers who wanted to join in began clapping. Mark and I hugged each other and stared and cooed at the child who was now our son. He wasn't just handsome; he was beautiful.

Like many Mexican-American babies, he had big brown eyes that had a slight slant to them, almost Asian in appearance. His gorgeous eyes were framed by an abundant supply of black eyelashes that were nearly as long as the bristles on paint brush. His complexion was a creamy light brown. He was wide awake and he stared back at us. He appeared to be staring straight into Mark's eyes. Despite all the excitement and noise, he was quietly checking us out. His eyes gravitated to his father's face and fixed there. We checked out his fingers and toes, an age-old ritual at deliveries from time immemorial. Everything was perfect, of course. He had a head of thick black hair. It was so thick that I wondered if he had been born with a full head of hair.

The feeling of love was like a surge. It was so strong that it was almost frightening. We had waited so long and I had often imagined this event, but nothing could compare to the way it felt. It was so intensely joyous that it seemed unreal. But it wasn't a dream—it was real. Everyone in our immediate entourage had held back, so now it was time to show our son to his relatives and friends. They all sang his praises. He now was in our care and he was our responsibility. It somehow seemed strange as his social worker and our social worker walked away. After all the scrutiny, the hoping you'll make the grade, your dependence on others to grant you your most important wish, it had finally happened! We had our son and the intermediaries were walking away. We were on our own. The difficult and painful process leading to adoption had resulted in this wonderful joy.

We celebrated for a week. Friends and relatives visited in the evenings to see our son and to celebrate with us. We named him Mark Tomas after his father and respecting his heritage. We thought he was amazing and that at fourteen weeks of age, he was already sleeping through the night. It wasn't until the bustle and celebration of that first week was over that we discovered he did indeed awake at both 1 am and 4 am.

We had spent so much time wishing to be parents, then trying to be parents, and then waiting to be parents until finally, we actually were parents. When Mark Tomas first arrived, our responsibility was initially a physical, custodial one. Overnight, it was overlaid with this awesome, emotional accountability. What he would become, in some degree would be due, at least in part, to our influence. And children, too, carry the responsibility to try and live up to their parent's expectations. Those expectations may be unsaid and/ or unconscious on the parent's part; nonetheless, some message is conveyed and inherent in the role of being someone's child.

Our lives revolved around him and we learned what being parent to an infant entailed. Mark was a good baby. He slept when he was supposed to, ate when we fed him, and he smiled. He was happy and alert. He did everything by the book. He smiled, rolled over, sat up, stood, crawled, walked, and said his first words when all the developmental books said he should be doing those things.

We started to forget the long wait for his arrival. The pain of not having a child was fading. The anxiety of the home study prior to his arrival was becoming a memory. My fears that we would be denied as adoptive parents now seemed ridiculous. And I had worried. My wish for a child was so consuming that even though I knew we should qualify as adoptive parents, my mind would conjure up all the unlikely reasons for our rejection.

Conversations about babies and baby showers no longer had to be avoided. The pains of my own personal experiences with childbearing were now behind me, so I was able to confront those memories rather than keeping them at a safe distance.

The reproductive experience was a painful one for both Mark and me. Becoming pregnant had been no problem, but I had had no success at carrying a baby to term. After one full-term stillbirth and three miscarriages, I had been afraid to go through all that again. But now, I had joined the ranks of all those other women. I was a mother!

The happiness Mark Tomas brought to us made us think more and more of expanding our family. To tell the truth, a part of me was scared by how intense my maternal feelings were for him—I felt maybe it needed to be diffused a little. What would I ever do if something should happen? What if my love was so strong that I could possibly harm him with its intensity? Wouldn't it be nice for Mark Tomas to have a brother or sister to grow up with? But the overriding reason to try again to have a child was his presence in our lives and all the love we shared. It enabled me to think about becoming pregnant in a positive light rather than with dread.

I did become pregnant in the fall of 1981and the following year did prove to be stressful. Visits to the high-risk clinic at St. Margaret's Hospital became part of my routine. Mark Tomas accompanied me to all those appointments for the first six months of my pregnancy. The doctor had assured me that if I could make it through the first thirteen weeks safely, they felt sure they could help carry me through the last two trimesters. I did make through the magic week thirteen and it was a go.

I was placed on a high-protein diet of 100 grams of protein a day. The thinking at that time was high protein for 'at risk' pregnancies would ensure an enriched placenta—thus optimum nutrition for the developing baby. It was no easy task to consume that amount of protein daily. At that time, professional football players were consuming 64 grams of protein a day. I was drinking shakes with protein powder, raw eggs, ice cream, and eating large portions of meat at lunch and dinner. Midway through the second semester, I was required to fill out a kick test daily.

I had to monitor fetal kicks for 30 minutes a day and needed to record at least sixteen kicks in that period. If that did not occur, I had to contact the high-risk clinic and come in for a non-stress test so they could determine that everything was OK and determine that the baby was not in distress. My anxieties and fears about the pregnancy were balanced with the pleasure I took in caring for Mark Tomas. I was able to make it through the third trimester with several non-stress tests and one stress test. Finally, after a nail-biting labor and delivery fraught with complications, Andrew was born on June 22, 1982. As Mark

Tomas's birthday was July 21, 1980, about to be two-years old, he now had a baby brother.

Shortly after discovering I was pregnant, I learned that my mother had been diagnosed with terminal colon cancer. Our routine during my pregnancy now included frequent trips to New York to spend time with my mother and father. Mark Tomas gave pleasure to my mom and dad and was a much-needed reminder that life goes on. He became adept at playing in hospital waiting rooms, and his energetic and social manner brought smiles to people in the waiting rooms often preoccupied with dark thoughts.

Five weeks prior to my due date, my mother died. I loved my mother and she was always easy to talk to about my concerns, thoughts, and feelings. But the last year had been agonizing. On each visit, her decline was obvious. Her entire life, she had been overweight. But in this last year, she shriveled up until there was almost none of her there. As she wasted away physically, she was also drifting in and out of a comatose-like state and her memory vacillated greatly. On one visit, she woke up to see me sitting on her bed and pronounced that the baby I was carrying was dead. She was reliving my past pregnancy, but despite my being aware of this, I worried that this was an omen. She was always tired to the point of exhaustion even though she was rarely out of bed.

On a following visit, she was alert and called my father and me together in her room. In the next hour and a half, she planned her funeral arrangements to the last detail and told us to make all the arrangements ahead of time so we did not have to do this at the last minute. We followed her instructions to the letter. After she died, we had time to mourn her, since all the arrangements were already in place. I missed her sorely, but I remember her mostly as she lived, not as she was in her final days. I had felt so helpless as her condition worsened for there was nothing I could do to make things easier for her. I knew that each day she lived, she would feel no better. She lives on in my memories and I still share experiences with her in my mind.

Mark Tomas' arrival switched my focus from a working woman to that of a young mother. I had the luxury of being able to take a hiatus from work during which I took the time to reflect on my new role: what were my expectations, my hopes, and my desires as a parent. And like most young adults, I would critique my parents' performance, using them to develop my own dos and don'ts list. From this came a tentative set of personal standards influencing how I would like to act as a parent. However, this microscopic inspection of their talents and flaws was viewed from the jaundiced eye of my childhood perceptions. As I grew into my role as a parent, I developed a greater sense of compassion and understanding of how great was the responsibility of caring for and loving a child.

Issues I previously thought were clearly black or white now looked grey to me. Stepping into their footsteps (now that I too was a parent) provided me with a new lens in which to view them. I felt that I was now judging them in retrospect more realistically as people rather than as my parents. This view had greater dimension as I was developing a sense of how multi-layered the role of parenting was. In some ways, this liberated my relationship with my mother and father. After my mother's death, I was so grateful that this changed perspective had come to pass. I could appreciate many of the things she and my father had done in a way I had not considered before. In another way, it was sometimes disappointing stepping back to see my parents in a different light in a more detached perspective.

Most difficult of all was a sense of disappointment for not being able to have seen my mother in the role of grandmother. I felt she would have enjoyed this role and that it would have brought to the forefront her finest traits. She was a great teacher and explainer. As a child, I vividly remembered a walk on the beach with her where she entertained me with her knowledge about all the things we discovered in our beach combing.

She did this with a sense of adventure and excitement, without even a hint of lecturing. I had always admired her astute perceptions about people and her ability to put people's actions in the context of their individual talents and limitations. She was able to put things in context and not take things personally where others might. It was a type of intellectual distance that served her well. She was my role model, and I am sure she was chagrined to see all her children inherit her capacity for analyzing people's behavior and use that ability to analyze and interpret her every move!

Her talent for dispassionate appraisal had less-welcome side effects, and I regretted that she was not more physically affectionate. I was always clear that she loved me, but there was a constriction in her behavior that I sensed—an emotional warmth that was lacking but more likely a feeling she was uncomfortable in expressing. I thought that if she had been given the opportunity to be a grandmother, she would finally have been able to express the warmth I was sure she felt. But perhaps this might be where my mother and I were essentially different. She could offer a reassuring word or consoling thought where I was always ready with a hug. So maybe even as a grandmother, she might have responded the same. Nonetheless, I would have liked the opportunity to have found this out.

Why was my mother distant in dealing with me and my brother and sister? I always thought that my mother carried within her a large suitcase of guilt. Despite her desire for a family, she was a career woman, a generation or two ahead of her time! She worked not only out of necessity but also out of need and felt guilty because of it. She knew few other mothers who were working and this affected her finding close relationships with other women. And I think this affected her self-confidence as a mother.

When I was in my twenties, I remember a conversation with her where she expressed her guilt about feeling that maybe her children had gotten the short end of the stick due to her need to work. She was a social worker and worked from the time her children began elementary school. She herself was the product of a working mother. My grandmother's husband died when her family was young. She put herself through college and graduate school at night and then worked full time. My grandmother was also a social worker. In fact, she was one of the first female Probation Officers in the city of New York. So, it is no surprise that my mom followed in her footsteps, as I have in hers. These apples didn't fall far from that tree!

She loved to cook and she passed that passion on to me. Many weekends, she would experiment using her extensive library of cookbooks making new meals and I would serve as her assistant. I remember one Mother's Day when I was a teenager using her cookbook to prepare a Mother's Day feast of

Beef Wellington and Pineapple Flambé for dessert. The only misstep in my meal preparation was that I did not burn off the alcohol content in the brandy sufficiently. The Pineapple Not Enough Flambé resulted in everyone getting buzzed! From both my mother and father, I received a sense of liberal ideals. They both felt a commitment to those who were less fortunate in society and passed those ideals on to their children. In their personal lives and in their work lives, they tried to help others. I was fortunate to have grown up having parents I admired. Their influence had played a big part in who I am as a person and in my different roles as wife, mother, and in my work life as first a social worker and later as a psychiatric nurse.

Fortunately for my children, I have internalized some of their good qualities as well as some of their less-than-ideal characteristics. What has continued to amaze me as I have grown older is the fact that while I may be working hard to alter my behavior in some areas, other traits seemed so ingrained in a part of me that I am at times totaly unaware of them. I have sometimes wondered if would be able to change them had I wished to do so. My relationship with my mother continues, for I have found that I have mental conversations with her, which helps me sort things out. And after these conversations, I feel relieved and supported. And the older I grow, the more I realize how much like her I really am.

After my mother had died, Mark's mother, Mimi, became my sage. She filled a large space in my heart that was vacant after my mother's death. When my children were young, I was able to share any concerns about them and she always helped me put things in perspective.

My close friend Debbie had a daughter within a year of Mark Tomas's arrival, and we both settled into a pleasant routine. We would get together several times a week with our babies. For the early years, our families did many activities together. As the children became older, Debbie and I took them on a number of trips. Her friendship has been a constant source of support and understanding for which I have been very grateful.

When Mark Tomas was nine months old, I returned to work part-time. I was able to find a job at a nearby private psychiatric hospital, which enabled me to tailor my hours that involved only a minimum of childcare. I was working Monday, Wednesday, and every other weekend, 3–11 shift on an adult, locked psychiatric unit. Four hours a day, two days a week, I would drop Mark off at a family daycare nearby and he had the opportunity to play with other children. I dropped him off at 2 pm and his father picked him up at 6 pm. In the beginning, I think my adjustment was as large as his was. I hated leaving him, but I believed there were benefits in his being with other children and in learning that each time I left, I always returned.

Now a year and a half later, he had a younger brother. Mark Tomas was ready to play with Andy, long before Andy was ready to play with him. I remember entering the living room one day to find Mark Tomas trying to play baseball with his baby brother. He had placed the ball in his brother's hands and was poised over the crib with a baseball bat waiting for Andrew to throw the ball to him. After my heart stopped bounding, I explained that babies were not ready to grasp the intricacies of baseball. I went on to say that baseball was an activity for him and his father! I now made the transition from mothering one child to trying to meet and balance the needs of two young children.

During Andrew's first month, he became ill. It was summer and our family had spent the afternoon at Mark's brother Dennis' pool. It was a fun afternoon and we all returned home tired. A few hours later, Andrew developed a fever. It spiked quickly and then I noticed that he was arching his back. I called our pediatrician and he said calmly to keep Andy in a diaper only and drive him in an air-conditioned car to Mass General Hospital (MGH). He said he would notify the hospital and that we were to bring him directly to the hospital. Mark called his father and he arrived in minutes with the air-conditioning blasting to drive us to the hospital. Mark's mother got out of the car and entered our house to look after Mark Tomas.

We arrived at MGH within 20 minutes; it was a weekend night so there was no traffic. Andrew was taken out of my arms and we were told to wait in the pediatric emergency lobby while they did some tests. We were able to hear Andy crying through the walls. Our pediatrician called and spoke with me. He said they would be doing a number of tests and he suspected that Andrew had contracted meningitis. We waited hours for an update and finally were told of a delay because some of the lab equipment was down and they had to wait for test results before they could make a diagnosis and treatment protocol. At 5 am, the emergency doctor came out and told us that they had confirmed the diagnosis of spinal meningitis. The head of the infectious disease department was on his way in and would meet with us on the Pediatric Unit as Andrew was being admitted there.

A few hours later, the Infectious Disease Chief Physician came in our room and introduced himself. He had gone over all the lab results and stated he could state with 95 percent confidence that the meningitis was viral not bacterial. He was discontinuing the antibiotics and the treatment would be a highly air-conditioned room and fluid restriction until the fever broke. He assured us that Andy would come out of this with no complications. Mark went home to relieve his mother. I stayed with Andy and shivered while I held him when he was not sleeping. Within 24 hours, the fever abated and he was cleared to go home and return to his normal diet. That was quite a scare!

After Andy was born, we began to think about moving to a larger home and also moving out of the city. We began house hunting on weekends. After a long time of exploring various suburban communalities, we found a house we liked and moved to Hingham, Massachusetts. When we made this move, Mark Tomas was six years of age and Andy was four. We were out of the city, able to access better public schools yet we were still a close distance to Mark's family. I obtained a part-time job at the same mental health center where I had worked earlier at the Day Treatment Center. This time, I would be working part-time for South Shore Mental Health Center as a Psychiatric Nurse for the Crisis Team.

Mark and I talked about having another child. After several discussions, we made the decision to seek out adoption again as a way to expand our family. Preferably, we would love to add a daughter to our family, but we were open to any child. We contacted The Alliance For Children and began the process of filling out the extensive application for the second time. We anticipated that the process would be the same as our experience had been with Mark Tomas.

We thought that a child would join our family in a year or more time in the future. We were told that if we were interested in another child, it was likely that infants would be placed with couples that had no children. We would more likely be considered for a child that was around two years of age or older. We felt that that was workable, but we felt we did not have the resources for a child with serious medical needs. In these early years, we were happy, we were busy, and we enjoyed the role of parenting as an integral part of our marriage.

I had just started my job on the crisis team and was replacing another psychiatric nurse who had gone out on maternity leave. Five weeks into this job, I received a phone call from our adoption worker. She reported that a baby girl had been born in Massachusetts and they were trying to find her a home. She went on to say that the girl was five weeks premature. She was initially placed in the Intensive Care Unit as she had a stroke within 24 hours of her birth, which was not uncommon with premature babies. She asked that Mark and I think about this and consult with our pediatrician. She felt that we were preferred over childless couples as I was a nurse and could evaluate her medical problem at birth, which the hospital felt was now stabilized.

Mark and I discussed this and decided that we would decide based on what our pediatrician could tell us. I contacted our pediatrician, Dr. Mark Vonnegut. He was willing to consult with the doctors at University of Massachusetts Medical Center Hospital (UMMC), where the baby was being treated. He had several phone calls to various doctors at UMMC and called us the following morning. His report was that the area of her brain that had suffered the stroke did not involve cognition.

His words were: "The area affected was one that has some control over physical responsiveness. She may never win medals as a long-distance runner, but that is the only thing she might never be able to do. She is stabilized and has normo-pressure hydrocephalus, which means she has some excess fluid in that area of her brain, which could resolve itself with no intervention. My opinion is that if you are looking to add a girl to your family, her problem at birth should not hold you back." Mark and I talked again and decided we were definitely interested in pursuing the adoption but resolved to sleep on it and make a decision in the morning.

I hardly slept that night and my initial nervousness about taking this on shifted to a growing excitement that I would be gaining a daughter. Mark agreed that we should go ahead, even though it was a year sooner than we expected to increase our family. I called the adoption worker and she estimated that our baby would be brought to us in a week's time.

In that time, we had to complete another home study, but she said she could use much of the information from our initial home study for our packet. Then I had the difficult task of talking with my new employer and telling him of our plan to adopt a child in a year's time had altered, as a baby was currently available. I asked if it was possible that I be granted a three-month maternity leave to start a week from our meeting. He conferred with his boss and the decision was made to hold my part-time position open and grant me the maternity leave without pay. Whew!

We had Mark's family over for a celebration and we got out the name book and everyone drew ballots of names they liked. Then we all voted on the top three favorites. Mark and I looked at them the next day and chose Beth Kathleen. Beth arrived one week later and this delivery took place in our driveway. My friend Debbie and Mark's mother and sister were also present—and of course so were Mark Tomas and Andrew. When the van came up the driveway, Mark and I went out to welcome our daughter home. Beth Kathleen was placed in our arms.

She had a fair complexion, and what hair she had, appeared to be red, and beautiful brown eyes. This time, our social worker said we would complete the paperwork on her next visit, the following week. I carried Beth in and first showed her to her brothers, then to the rest of our family and my friend. I should mention that Beth had follow-up care at Mass General Hospital's Pediatric Neurology Department for the next two years until her condition was totally resolved and she needed no further assessments. Even more wonderful was the fact that she turned out to be a fantastic athlete and played on high school varsity teams for basketball, soccer, and softball!

Chapter 9
1986 – 1992: Trouble Brewing

When did I realize that we might have trouble ahead? To be honest, every once and a while, from early on, I would get an uncomfortable twinge when Mark Tomas seemed to me to be overly upset about a particular situation. I'd get this sick feeling in the pit of my stomach or sometimes my heart would race. It wasn't what he was saying: "You can't make me. I won't do it. I hate you"—it was the intensity of the outburst and shift from calm to anger in less than a nanosecond. The incident would blow over and I would move on, glad to put the from calm to 60-shift uncomfortable sensation behind.

And to be fair, there were times when he had a right to be upset. But at other times, his anger was out of proportion to the situation. After each episode, I would explain to him that life is complicated; things are never black or white. Mark and I would rehash what had happened and come up with a list of reasons to explain why the situation didn't turn out as we expected. We called them 'mitigating factors'.

In nursery school, when he became unhappy, the teacher was a mitigating factor. She didn't get on well with the four-year-old boys; this was also the consensus of the parents of the boys in her class. But Mark Tomas refused to go along with her directions. He would walk around the room aimlessly; I think it was an attempt to avoid all interaction with her.

He never complained or gave us any indication that he was unhappy. After the teacher told us she felt he was immature because he seemed unable to focus on a task and carry it out, then we began to question him more closely about school. He continued to deny that there was any problem though he did not look happy when talking about his mornings there. When he finally did 'spill the beans', it was to a neighbor, not to us. He told this neighbor that he hated the teacher but could not give any reasons why this was so.

In both the first and second grade, he would have major temper tantrums over our trying to help him with his homework. He would initially let me look at his homework and begin to go over it with him. After about five minutes' time, he would become frustrated, then start throwing his books on the floor, then turn over chairs and start yelling. His face would get red and his facial expression was one of anger.

His anger only dissipated when he was reduced to tears. We could understand that he was frustrated. We suspected that he was having difficulties with learning. When we went over his homework at night, he would master it; yet when we reviewed it in the morning, he had absolutely no recollection of it. It was all a blank. It was as if he had not studied it at all, yet we knew he had, and that he had understood it the previous evening.

Our strategy was to keep an eye on this and monitor his progress. We gave him plenty of positive feedback for his persistence despite his frustration. His anger seemed appropriate to the context; it was just a matter of degree. Sometimes, the anger flew into a rage. It frightened us, so we could only imagine how terrified he must be with these losses of control. It was hard to know at times, whether we were seeing fierce independence or defensiveness.

In the early years, the anger was episodic interspersed with periods of gentleness, concern for others, humor and insight that seemed beyond his years. When we moved to Hingham, Mark Tomas finished his last six weeks of kindergarten in the local elementary school. After first grade, we decided to have him repeat the year to give him some more time to mature. His teacher advised us to do this stating an additional year would help give him more time to focus.

When Mark Tomas was nine years old, he had a very difficult year. He had a terrible experience with his third-grade teacher. She seemed to delight in putting him down and in pointing out his every weakness. She seemed unable to see any of his good points. Dealing with her was enraging for us, his parents. How could we expect him to remain calm in the face of this constant erosion of his self-confidence? We attended a number of school conferences that year, but little was accomplished. His teacher was unyielding. She would make no accommodations or try a different approach with him.

I have regretted that we did not force the issue and insist that he be moved to another classroom. It did motivate us to go outside the school system to have Mark Tomas evaluated. And our suspicions that he was dealing with underlying problems were confirmed. We had him evaluated at New England Medical Center, in the neurology department. He was diagnosed with multiple learning difficulties. It was no wonder that he was frustrated beyond belief!

Learning of his difficulties created a mix of emotions. Our hearts ached for him. It seemed so unfair that he should have such a difficult time of it. We loved him so much and we anguished over his having these major obstacles to overcome. We were also relieved. Here was something real to get a hold on—there was a reason for his struggling with schoolwork and his obvious frustration. Our perceptions that he was a smart boy were also borne out by the testing. We were told that he had average to above average intelligence.

He was diagnosed with deficits in memory storage and retention, auditory processing and retention, attention deficit disorder, graphomotor disorder, and impulse control disorder. We were also told that he had difficulty managing his anger. I dealt with the news by trying to become a mini expert on learning difficulties, attention deficit disorder, and different learning styles. I read books and tried to both understand and to advocate for him. It was suggested that Mark could benefit from therapy to help him manage his feelings and frustration. I had the recommendations from the NEMC's evaluation incorporated into his Individualized Educational Plan.

We started him in therapy with a child psychologist, which was also a recommendation of the evaluation. By the end of the year, things appeared to have simmered down to our relief. Did the therapy help? It was hard to measure. Mark Tomas had someone who was supportive, caring, and who played to his strengths. He never protested going to the appointments, but he was never really enthusiastic either. The psychologist told us nothing we did not already know. It certainly did no damage, but no great strides were made either. He was very traditional and shared very little information with us about the therapy.

Seeking therapy for your child is an unnerving process. When you decide to enter therapy for yourself, you may be a little self-conscious and wary. But it is difficult not to be defensive when you seek therapy for your child. The initial interview brings out your worst fears; that you will be found lacking in some ways as a parent. In defense of child therapists, they need to ask questions to find out what is going on, and they certainly have heard terrible stories of abuse and neglect.

After some basic questions, things heat up with specific questions. Do you drink? Do you use drugs? Do you have a mental illness for which you have been or are being treated? How do you set limits? What was your childhood experience? Has your child been traumatized or abused in any way? Despite knowing intellectually that these questions need to be asked, it is hard not to feel judged. It takes courage to pursue this avenue for your child. Your privacy is peeled away, and it takes skill and finesse as a therapist to put parents at ease in a therapeutic environment.

I have thought often that some child therapists are so child-centered that they inadvertently do a disservice to parents. The skill in which the first interview is conducted sets a tone for parents that may take months to overcome. I got through the first interview by telling myself: "Relax, once he gets to know you and understands the situation, he'll get to know that we are good people". For I did feel that in some way I was being judged, and it is hard to develop trust when you feel that you are being examined.

God knows you are bringing feelings of insecurity and failure as a parent along with you to the interview. Your child is hurting, or you wouldn't be there in the first place. And most parents feel guilty or responsible when their child is hurting. You feel like you should have been able to prevent it. You have already second-guessed yourself to death before you arrive at the therapist's door. Hopefully, any therapist worth his or her salt tries to establish some rapport with you over time, and it gets easier and easier to enter that office.

Another consideration with child therapy is the parent's need for feedback. Unless parents are part of the process and are consulted and advised, it's unlikely that much change will take place. I think therapists forget that parents also feel vulnerable and need reassurance as well as the child. They depend on the parent to offer their perceptions of what the problems are and to give progress reports on how the child is doing from session to session. Why should parents expect any less from the therapist? If the tone is set from the beginning that we are all working together to make things better, then there is a way to be open in giving and receiving information about the child and the family.

Despite our concerns over Mark Tomas' challenges in school and his difficulty managing anger at times, other aspects of his life were going well. He was active in sports; he was playing soccer, baseball, and hockey. Since he and Andy were only two years apart, every other year they were on the same teams. As parents, Mark and I were avid fans and enjoyed watching the children's games. Mark coached his soccer and baseball teams for a number of years. Mark Tomas had lots of friends and socialized after school. He had shown a real talent for drawing and could occupy himself sketching with paper and pencil. He also had a talent for taking things apart and then putting them back together. He had a routine where he liked his father to read to him at bedtime. Most of the time, he appeared to be happy.

His adoption was brought up often, and was a basic, open fact from the start of our family. We talked of the joy his adoption brought to us. We stressed how fortunate we felt to be our own blended family and how his cultural heritage broadened us and widened our horizons. We called him affectionate and playful nicknames when he was a toddler. He was our 'Mexican jumping bean'. After Mark and I read the book Taipei, we called him 'Marco-san' for a while.

We tried to have more serious talks also. We would ask him if he ever thought about his adoption. Did he think about his biological mother? Were there any questions he had or would like answers to? He never admitted to thinking about his background. We told him most of what little we knew about his mother. And we did have very little information. Whenever we tried to explore his feeling about this, he generally put us off.

In fact, I would come away from these attempts at discussion feeling like I was trying to force something down his throat, and I would quickly back off the topic. I would leave feeling that this was my agenda, not his. Then I would tell myself to leave it alone until he was ready to talk and appeared more approachable. I naively thought it wasn't on his mind; I took him at his word. I thought to myself that I must be rushing things and that this would become more important to him in his teen years. Big mistake! We would learn this only too well in later years.

Our lives were busy and full. We had good days and bad ones, but the good days far outnumbered the bad. We had a routine. I was working part-time and we had a baby-sitter who cared for Beth and watched the boys after school until I arrived home. It was a good year. Mark Tomas had a wonderful teacher in the fourth grade. Mrs. Kirby really enjoyed him and played to his strengths. She quickly perceived that he had good abstract reasoning skills and that he was catching on to those concepts before many other kids in the class. She would call on Mark Tomas to explain these concepts to the class. She was very open and told the class that she had Attention Deficit Disorder.

She talked a lot about different learning styles and used a variety of teaching techniques in her classroom. Her room was a beehive of activity. It was noisy and messy, but those children worked, had fun, and produced large amounts of work. She was a pleasure to work with and she tried to learn as much as she could about each child in her classroom. Mark Tomas blossomed under her tutelage. He was producing 'A' quality work and enjoying it. We were so grateful for the wonderful experience Mark had that year that I wrote letters to the Superintendent of Schools and to her School principal praising her and the influence she had on our son. That school year went well and not surprising, it was a calm year at home also.

Andrew was in second grade and was a boisterous flurry of activity. He could not sit still. He was rarely silent. He was very verbal and had a large vocabulary. By the age of four, he had picked up his father's favorite way to begin a sentence. All his sentences started with either 'perhaps' or with 'actually'! If he thought it, he said it. He could race from one thing to another and it was difficult to keep up with him. He was very affectionate and his emotions were right there on the surface for all to see. His idea of hell was having nothing to do. Countless times, I would hear him refrain: "What can I do now, Mom?" Every afternoon, he had activities planned with different school friends. His endless socializing led us to give him the nickname: 'The mayor of Hingham'. He was enthusiastic and loved to make people laugh. He was very popular with his classmates because he was such fun to be with.

The boys were such a contrast. Mark Tomas was quiet, stoic and kept things close to his chest. Yet, it was clear that he had astute perceptions about people. He was also adept about identifying in adults their vulnerable or weak spots. He knew how to get under their skin. While this is a sophisticated skill, it is a dual-edged sword as having this ability is frequently found in an adult sociopath. At the time, I perceived he had this skill, he was in first or second grade. So, I did not connect it with any forewarning of future development. Younger children gravitated to him. He was gentle and understanding with them. On the school bus, the first-grade boys would argue over who would sit next to him. Parents would tell me that their sons had strong cases of hero-worship for Mark. Andrew looked up to his older brother and respected him. Their love of sports gave them a common ground.

Beth adored her brothers. She too had boundless energy and wanted to join them in everything they did. She loved physical activity and would play with them whether or not they desired her presence. She could never comprehend that they were older and might want to do things without her. She was hard to ignore, and if they left her out of a basketball game, she was undaunted in her attempts to join the fun. She would stay and wait for her opportunity to grab the ball and shoot hoops anyway. On countless occasions, I would hear: "Mom, make Beth go in the house. We're trying to have a game of basketball!" I felt I needed the wisdom of Solomon, trying to balance the boys' need to play together with her need to be included.

In the fifth grade, Mark Tomas again had difficulties at school. He was in the regular classroom for most of the day, but he was assigned to the resource room for one hour a day and here he received individual attention from the resource room teacher and her assistant. She was a good advocate for Mark and attended all the school conferences and IEP (Individualized

Education Plan) meetings. Mark Tomas resented being sent to the resource room. He rarely completed his homework and whether he did it or not, he never handed it in. His locker was stocked with past-due homework assignments. When asked if he had homework, he often lied and told us either he had already done it or that he had no homework.

He began stealing money from his dad and I, and then from his brother and sister. Items he coveted would disappear. I developed an insane rule, telling his brother and sister that if they had something that was really important to them, they should change their hiding place for these items every three weeks! We never saw Mark Tomas actually take the items, but we knew that he was responsible for their disappearance. What did his brother and sister think? They loved him, they got annoyed with him, they watched his meltdowns with some degree of confusion, but they knew nothing different. He was their brother and sometimes he had temper tantrums and sometimes he took things that didn't belong to him.

In school that year, his class was team-taught. I had monthly conferences to monitor Mark's progress. These conferences included his three teachers and Mark Tomas and me. When this proved insufficient to keep on top of his assignments, his resource room teacher and I would communicate weekly by phone regarding work that was due to be turned in to his teachers.

One episode at home occurred when he and Beth were watching TV and they began arguing over what TV show to watch. Mark Tomas became angry that Beth wasn't agreeing with his choice and he threw the TV remote control at her with force. It hit her in the face and chipped her front two teeth leaving a gaping hole in her mouth. Beth was beside herself and insisted she would not return to school until her teeth were fixed. I called the dentist the following morning and reported that Beth needed to be seen to repair these two teeth. The dental assistant told me her earliest appointment was the following week! I refused to be put off and said that she had to be seen that day. After much back and forth, I was begrudgingly given an appointment for later that afternoon.

During this year, we switched therapists, and Mark Tomas began seeing a therapist whose specialty was boys with

Attention Deficit Disorder. This therapist put Mark Tomas in a group of boys of similar age who also had been diagnosed with ADD. He liked this group and this therapist. Tim was very helpful to us. He advocated on Mark's behalf at school conferences. He was down to earth and gutsy, so the boys had an easy time confiding in him. He felt strongly that Mark Tomas needed a consult with a child psychiatrist who was familiar with ADD and who would evaluate him for medication. We pursued this and Mark Tomas was evaluated and started on Ritalin. I had high hopes that medicine would be a value-added tool in our toolbox.

As a psychiatric nurse, I had high exposure to people on meds and often saw a night and day difference in patient's behavior once they were stabilized on a particular medication regime. Mark reported that the medication made it easier for him to pay attention in school and that he felt less irritable. He was still having angry outbursts, usually in response to our confronting his behavior or our setting limits on him. Tim, his psychologist, explained that Mark had a very short fuse and had little advance warning when he was going to blow. He did feel that Mark did have some warning when he was starting to escalate. He worked with Mark in identifying signs when he was becoming irritated.

He felt Mark had five to ten second window before the anger took over, and he tried to implement a variety of steps for us to take when Mark Tomas was angry. We were instructed to give Mark Tomas two warnings when we felt he was starting to escalate or when he was verbally abusive. After the third incident, he was to go to his room to cool down. He also had the choice to go to the playroom in the basement and play Nintendo to calm. If he failed to comply, then we were to set a consequence. The consequence would vary depending on the seriousness of the offence. If he was verbally abusive and was cursing at me without heeding the warnings, then he might be grounded for a day. (He was very verbally abusive to me and would call me various monikers such as a f... bitch, a f... c... a f... whore, etc.) A less serious offense might warrant one hour in his room.

This was only partially effective for he was often testing the limits and it was an ordeal to implement them as he often refused to go to his room or the playroom. He was now in the fifth grade, he was not a toddler. I could not just pick him up and take him to his room. I was caught in a bind. Setting limits often escalated the situation but not setting limits was encouraging negative behavior.

I felt we needed to have some basic expectations for behavior. We had good weeks and weeks that were very difficult. We had long ago learned that the start and end of every school year was a difficult time for him. His particular class was a precocious one and started the girl-boy thing early. Girls were calling the house on a regular basis. The parties were girl-boy parties and he resented my calling the parent of the child holding the party to make sure that they would be home and supervising the children.

This was a common practice and other parents were doing the same checking that I was doing. At this point in time, Mark would get frustrated at Mark Tomas's outbursts. He would wait until it was over and Mark Tomas had moved on to some other task and then he would voice his displeasure to me. I understood, it was frustrating and it was upsetting but venting his displeasure onto me as his listening audience was stressful. I remember once discussing this with my mother-in-law that I was stressed by Mark Tomas becoming angry and then my having to listen to his father become angry and venting to me.

She told me that I needed to help Mark by being supportive and listening to his anger. I told her that I felt there was just too much anger to go around and it just seemed to me that this venting was not helpful or productive. She again stressed that I needed to be supportive and let my husband vent his emotions as a supportive wife. I felt let down. In my mind, if Mark Tomas was escalating, then remaining calm and not adding more intense emotions into the mix seemed a more constructive response. And I didn't see myself as a repository for other people's negative emotions, even if it was my husband.

Mark continued to be active in sports, and he and Andy were very good hockey players. So between town teams and AA teams, they played hockey ten months of the year as well as baseball and soccer. He took guitar lessons for about two years but lost interest, as the instructor was quite rigid and denied his requests to learn some modern music. Despite his talent for drawing, he always hated the art classes at school. He found the assignments tedious. He liked sketching animals and cartoons and machines. I would buy him drawing books, and he would copy in exact detail the objects on the pages. He loved school projects that allowed him to use his drawing talents as part of the class projects where he could build dioramas or sets using his own creativity.

The summer after fifth grade, we began to notice that Mark was balking at doing things as a family. He would ask to stay home if we were going to the harbor to have a picnic for dinner. When we insisted that he join us, he was angry and unpleasant. Sometimes, he would intentionally start a fight with his brother; sometimes, he would tease his sister. If he wasn't successful in getting us to change our minds, then he would refuse to get in the car. When he did begrudgingly join us, his displeasure cast a pall on our enjoyment. He began sulking more and talked to us less and less.

Sixth grade was a disaster academically but less of a problem behaviorally. Mark's teacher was having a difficult time with his own personal problems and had very little energy left to manage the class. Little work was done and it was clear that he had no control over the class. The situation deteriorated as the year went on. In the spring, the teacher lost control in the classroom. Rumor was that he physically manhandled a boy in the class. This rumor proved true as we knew the parents of the boy involved.

The teacher went out on leave and a substitute was brought into the class for the remainder of the school year. The result was that the entire class was unprepared for the transition to the Junior High the following fall. Despite this, I was looking forward to a change from the elementary school. I hoped this would be a positive new start for Mark Tomas and he was looking forward to moving up to the Junior High.

Mark and I were not looking for trouble. We viewed life as having its ups and downs. We lived in the present and had busy active schedules with all three children playing multiple sports with practices and games. Were we wearing rose-colored glasses? I honestly don't know. When problems emerged, we tried to deal with them. We had consulted experts and were trying to follow their advice. When things calmed down, we moved on. But having a child with severe emotional outbursts that were increasing in frequency and intensity was putting a stress on our marriage.

Looking back now, I can see that patterns were emerging. A recurring theme was Mark Tomas' difficulty dealing with perceived rejection with an angry response. He went from being quiet and reticent to having explosive outbursts. His being quiet and reticent was not being withdrawn and isolative. And angry outbursts were just that—outbursts, not a constant state. He was a child going through stages of development and he had the added burden of a number of learning disabilities, and he was transracial in a lily-white family.

Hingham was also a lily-while town. The majority of the transracial families were adoptive families. But I did not pick up on any racial bias. He never indicated that anyone had called him names. We also had shared many happy times, which counterbalanced the difficult ones. I was consistent in keeping in touch with his therapist, Tim, and his psychiatrist. During this time frame, he did have a number of medication changes and additions. Prozac had been added as had Clonidine as tools that might help his irritability and mood.

I remember in elementary school, one of his teachers gave an assignment for the children to do a family tree. This is a big issue for adopted kids. When we discussed the assignment, I asked Mark Tomas what he wanted to do. I gave him options. "Mark, you could do our present family tree, or we could work on a blended family tree with you having two mothers or you could do your fantasy family tree and put whoever you want on that tree." He chose option #3. He put his father as Michael Jorden, his uncle as Bobby Orr, he put another uncle as Michael Jackson! I sent a note in attached to the assignment, explaining the issue and his result.

The reality was that it was impossible to stay focused on one child for very long. There were three children with different needs, requirements, and schedules. Our routine left little breathing time at the end of the day. One day flew by after another. We led a hectic lifestyle with both parents working, three children in school with after-school activities, dinner, homework, some TV, and bedtime. Weekends were filled with sports activities. I could barely find time to clean the house. I was a minority of one, when it came to valuing the importance of being organized. I was barely keeping my head above water in the never-ending struggle to put things in their proper place and to have the house appear uncluttered, if not clean. My housemates tended to view my preoccupation with picking-up as slightly obsessive, while I viewed their dropping their belongings at random as disorganized and chaotic.

Chapter 10
1992 – 1993: Living in Crisis

The storm arrived with an adolescent burst as Mark Tomas entered the Junior High School. He was very eager to be leaving elementary school and he undoubtedly saw this as a step towards more independence. The previous summer, he had been moody. He socialized less with friends and hung around the house a lot of the time. He seemed directionless and was not open to any of our suggestions for keeping busy. Although he was at home, he really did not want to spend time with us. And at this point, we did not push it.

Once he latched on to the idea to be disruptive, he was a master at it and pursued this objective with a vengeance. There had been more than a few times that summer when he lost control and truth be told so did I. It is hard not to get sucked in to someone's anger when they are shouting obscenities at you. And if I did succeed to ignore his tirade, it infuriated him further. On two occasions, after repeated warnings, we actually let him out of the car to walk home. This was what he wanted, but he was furious nonetheless. It was a long, hot summer.

When Mark and I had time to talk, we invariably talked about our worries and concerns about Mark Tomas. It was clear our 'behavioral system' was not effective. This had been clearly set up with him and his therapist. The problem with the system was that Mark Tomas needed to buy into the system for it to have any chance of working. After the second warning, we were to set a consequence. We did this and he would want to debate the issue, explain his point of view, clarify the consequence, argue with the consequence, and ultimately defy it. It was often futile and frustrating.

Mark and I had very different styles, but at this point, our approaches became more blended. He tended to mull things over, while I was able to make decisions quickly. He was reticent, where I tended to jump right in to things. He was more abstract where I was very concrete. He would talk around an issue, where I would get right to the point. He was more patient than I was and he was a better explainer. He was a better teacher to the children. I was better at supporting them emotionally and better at reading their emotional cues. I was more flexible generally and less tied to tradition. But we had learned, during this phase, that before either of us committed ourselves to a course of action, we now automatically responded: "What did your father/mother say about this?"

The reality was that we were getting worn down emotionally. Mark and Mark Tomas became more distant with one another. And I fell into the role of becoming their conduit to one another as well as the filter of what they conveyed to each other. I took on this role to keep the peace. I felt that Mark Tomas had become adept at baiting his father and provoking him to anger. They would both dig in their heels and compromise became more difficult.

Mark Tomas had always been ambivalent about taking medication. He had been prescribed Ritalin and Prozac, but his compliance was inconsistent. He did not out-right refuse to take medication. He would accept his medication from me each morning and take it in front of me. Often, I would suspect he was not really taking it because he seemed so irritable and explosive. I would go on a house search and find pills everywhere. They were behind his bed, in his bed, in his bureau drawers, under pillows on the couch in the family room, and downstairs in the playroom.

I was perplexed as to how he was doing this since I was watching him carefully when he took his medication in front of me. I found out later from Andy. Andy related how Mark Tomas told him that even with mouth checks, he could find places in his mouth to store the pills so that I would not see them. Then he would move them stealthily with his tongue to another area of his mouth as I was checking on him. By far, his most ingenious feat, (confided to his brother) was how he could store a length of dental floss in his mouth prior to my giving him his pills. He would use his tongue to adhere the pill to the hidden string and would use his teeth to press down on the other end of the string. He would then swallow the pill in front of me and when I left the room, he would use his hand to grab the loose end of the string and slowly pull the pill back up from his throat and take it out of his mouth! Considering the great lengths to which he was willing to go to, we could not count on medication offering us much assistance in our struggle to find ways to help Mark Tomas calm down.

This was the backdrop for everyone's hopes and expectations as he started Junior High. It started with a bang. The first day of school, Mark brought home a new friend. They left school early, then came to our house and began drinking liquor from our liquor cabinet and proceeded to get drunk. Things were not off to a good start. I thought to myself: *The first day of middle school, something he had been waiting for and this is the result?* I was so disappointed. I think it dawned on me that hoping for a fresh start was just another unrealistic fantasy on my part. But on the other hand, as a mother, you just can't give up hope when your child is a young teenager. The first and most obvious change was that Mark developed an entire new set of friends. None of them lived near us. They were children who were bussed in as part of a METCO program.

The Metropolitan Council for Educational Opportunity is an educational non-profit in Massachusetts started in 1966. The program was designed to give children in areas where the schools were not up to par, an opportunity for a better education in a suburban school. The reality was also that almost all of these children were black with a few Asian children mixed in. We encouraged Mark Tomas to bring these friends home so we could get to know them. He did, on a very few occasions, bring home one or two of the boys. At first, they seemed pleasant, but as time went on, it was hard to approve of them since they were all getting in trouble together. And sometimes, Beth would report to me that he was with a fairly large group of boys who were roaming around town. This was the perfect battleground for a parent-adolescent war. It was quickly clear that if Mark Tomas had to choose between parents or peers, it would be peers.

School was not going well. Mark appeared to have given up. He never brought home books, he never had homework papers, and he never studied for tests. When we offered to help him with homework assignments, we were met with an adamant refusal. I was called to school several times that year. Usually, the offense was described as an 'attitude problem'. He would be rude to a teacher and would be defiant when limits were set. Mark and I had given the school permission to talk with his therapist and for his therapist to communicate with the school. Mark Tomas was becoming more defiant at home. He would stay out late on weekends and often not tell us where he was going. I was convinced that his adolescent rebellion was extreme and atypical in its defiance. He did make it through seventh grade.

That summer was awful. He was angry most of the time. He was also not making any attempt to accommodate us. His rages grew in frequency and were most often directed at me. A new behavior was that he was now being nasty to his brother and sister. He made no attempt to curb his language, which became very foul. He took on the persona of a gang member. He loved rap music and took on its pattern of speech. He identified with inner-city youth and took on the negative characteristics of this stereotype. He was saying clearly that he was different from us, as different as night and day.

For a number of years, money would go missing in our home. Sometimes, I would get to work and find that I had no money in my pocketbook. Beth and Andy would report that their money was missing. We suspected Mark and when he was asked about it, he became indignant. We did not catch him in the act, so we could not prove it. Now things were more extreme. I began to sleep with my pocketbook next to my bed. The rest of us found that our bureau drawers had been gone through and things were moved around. My gold chains had disappeared.

The first day of eight grade, Mark Tomas did not come home from school. I called some of his friends, but there was no answer. And we had no contact information of the METCO children with whom he was spending time. When it became evening, I widened my search and called more people. I learned that he was seen near one of the other schools at the other end of town. I got in my car and went looking for him. I did find him at that school with four other boys. He was drunk and staggering. For the past year, we had suspected he was drinking and probably using drugs, but he denied it. We had already emptied our liquor cabinet.

The first two months of eight grade, he was suspended three times. I was making frequent trips to school to pick him up to bring home for disciplinary reasons. He was being abusive to his teachers. He was intimidating other students. He had developed this mean, machismo stance. He was only fourteen years of age, but now, he was accepting no limits from us. If I told him to go to his room to calm down, he would walk out of the house. He was raging at me on a daily basis and calling me terrible names—sometimes just because I said good morning. He began to take on a threatening posture when he interacted with me. And he was making verbal threats to harm me. His father would become so upset by this behavior and his lack of respect, that he was becoming increasingly angry. So, I began to downplay these incidents. I would not tell him of things Mark had done.

I felt having two people angry was just making things worse not better. And I did not tell him that I was becoming afraid of my son. I did tell Mark Tomas' therapist of these incidents. He was now seeing Mark Tomas and myself in emergency sessions weekly, in addition to Mark's group therapy. Mark Tomas stayed out all night several times and Mark drove all over town checking out eight graders' homes to see if anyone knew where he was. There were times that we knew that people were covering for Mark Tomas. We were all living on the edge. Mark Tomas was out of control. Mark and I were nervous and edgy. Andy and Beth were afraid to bring anyone over to our house. We became more isolated as a family. It was a small town and we suspected Mark Tomas' behavior was being discussed at many a dinner table.

It was an awkward situation. People do not want to be intrusive, and they do not know what you know, so they do not say anything. We became self-conscious. We were stressed. These horrible things were happening within our family and we were powerless to stop them. Mark Tomas was barely keeping his head above water, and some days, I felt like I was drowning with him. We were angry with Mark Tomas, but more than that, we were heartsick. We were afraid that we had failed him in some major way, but we were too guilty to discuss our fears. And if that load of guilt was not enough, we were also guilty that Mark Tomas was using up so much of our time and energy that we were not giving enough to Andy and Beth. We were piling load upon load of guilt on our shoulders. It didn't help to know that guilt is not a productive emotion. It was there, and we were mired in it.

By this time, we had made serious alterations to our lifestyle. We had past the point of picking our battles. We were in reaction mode. It was like living in a war zone with grenades exploding around us. Mark's rage now appeared not tied to any precipitant. It was a constant. I knew his rage at me was totally disproportionate to anything I had done. In my gut, I suspected that the rage directed at me was displaced and really belonged to someone else. We had tried to talk about the adoption issue and how it might be playing a part in his identity problem. He consistently denied it. But his actions spoke volumes. After one particularly vitriolic assault on my character, I retorted: "This anger isn't meant for me, it's for your other mother! I'm the one who stuck by you, loved you, and raised you." There was no response.

I was living in outright fear now. Mark had progressed from verbal abuse to physical acts of violence. On one occasion, when I told him he could not go out, he picked up a frying pan of hot bacon and grease, and came after me with it. Despite my fear, I felt it was imperative to act calm. I backed away and told him to put down the frying pan in a firm manner. Andy was present and he started to approach Mark in an attempt to protect me. I told Andy not to worry; everything would be all right. Mark Tomas did put down the pan and stormed out to his room, slamming doors, and knocking down anything that was in his path.

On another occasion, Mark Tomas, Andy, and I were inadvertently locked out of the house. The boys were trying windows to see if one was unlocked.

Mark quickly became frustrated and said: "I'm gonna bash a window with this baseball bat".

I said: "No, Mark, I want to try some more to see if we can get in without doing any damage. Let's check other windows to see if they are unlocked".

He proceeded to argue with me. Andy told him to "knock it off" and then they began to argue. He became threatening and they began to hit one another.

Andy got in at least one good punch before I could stop them and this further infuriated Mark Tomas. He came at me with the baseball bat and taunted me that he could easily hit me. He had a frightening look on his face as he approached. Again, though I was scared to death, I pretended I was calm and flatly told him to put down the bat. He put it down and took off and did not come back till later that night. Andy and I somehow managed to get into the house without breaking a window. We must have located an open window somewhere on the first floor.

How did I manage to appear calm in these situations? At some point, I had one of those 'aha moments'. I recalled my father becoming ridiculously upset that my mother had neglected to buy some item on the shopping list. He began harping on this and becoming frustrated then angry, I remember my mother left the kitchen and closed herself in her bedroom to get some space from this tirade. Then my sister also retreated to our bedroom. I was left in the kitchen and I just stood there saying nothing but listening until he ran out of speed and calmed down. I remember at one point, my sister, brother, and I discussing how in our adult lives, we had all been involved in relationships where the other person had issues with anger and our baggage somehow drew us to those people. So, I had some early practice learning how to stare down anger face to face— no matter what I was experiencing internally.

Another time, he was upset with me when I confronted him on his verbal abuse towards me, and he began shoving me all over the family room. He would hold up his fist as if he was going to punch me and use his other arm to push me across the room. He did this several times before he released my arm so I could move away from him. Most of these incidents occurred after school. If Mark Tomas appeared angry and was directing it at me, Andy became reticent about meeting his friends, as he was worried about me.

I had developed a routine with Beth. If Mark Tomas was escalating, she was to leave the house and go to her friend, Louis' house, down the street, until I called her to come home.

One of the more frightening experiences for me was an incident where Mark Tomas' anger appeared icy cold and he held his fist in front of my face, taunting me by stating: "I could smash you in the face and do some serious damage if I wanted to". I moved back and told him to stop. He continued to approach me and put his fist in front of my face. I realized that I was in the same situation as that of a battered wife. If my husband was doing this, I would have made him leave with no questions asked. But this was my son.

In my heart, I knew from that September that things would come to a head. And that I would have to make the most awful decision a mother can make. I would be forced to tell Mark Tomas he could no longer live in our home behaving like he was behaving. I knew this with my head, but my heart kept hoping against hope that it wouldn't come to pass. I was feeling shell-shocked. I had a hard time concentrating. I became very anxious. And I began to cry whenever I talked about what was happening.

I was crying in my sleep and waking up with swollen eyes. I was unable to get any respite from the stress and the fear. I became depressed. My friends at work took me aside and told me it was time for me to see a psychiatrist for meds to get me through this difficult time. They recognized that I began to cry whenever anyone mentioned Mark Tomas. I, who was always so solution-focused, could not solve this problem. I did see a psychiatrist and he recommended that I start on Prozac. I did and I remained on this medication for eleven months. I did stop crying. I was calmer, but I cared about everything less while I was on the medication. I developed a much larger appetite (most people lose weight) and I gained fifty pounds in that eleven months. It got me through the crisis, but the side effects were a high price to pay.

Mark was also very upset at what was happening. He was never home when these incidents occurred. On the one hand, I was glad for I felt that if he witnessed Mark Tomas' threatening me, he could get so angry that he could lose control. And then I would have two people who were out of control to worry about what could occur. It was easier for Mark to express anger about what was happening to our family than to express sadness. But on the other hand, I was resentful that I was getting the major brunt of all of this rage. And since by this time, he was getting so angry when I talked about this with him, I kept things to myself and became even more resentful.

We had become dysfunctional. Mark and I were unable to share our pain with each other and we became distant. And we could see signs in our other children that showed us that they were suffering also from this ongoing stress. Mark and I did have an unemotional conversation and were able to share that we both agreed that we were at the end of our ropes. We were not able to share deeper emotions, but we knew we had reached the limit. Things could not go on like this any longer.

We told Mark Tomas that if his behavior continued, we would have to take steps to end it, that the situation was now beyond our ability to manage.

We had several conversations that played out the same. We would sit down and say: "Mark Tomas, things cannot go on this way any longer."

He would respond: "Are you throwing me out?"

We would counter: "No, you will always be part of this family, but this can't continue and we will do whatever it takes to get you the help that you need."

We loved him, but we no longer trusted him. We were exhausted. We knew he needed help—the whole family needed help—but we did not know where to turn. Mark Tomas's therapist still seemed to think that we could reach Mark and that he would be able to turn things around. My heart so wanted to believe this, but I knew we had about reached the point of no return.

Chapter 11
1993: The Break

Mark Tomas's therapist began to talk of the need for residential placement. We sent away for a brochure for one place that specialized in Attention Deficit Disorder. They had no openings and did not expect one until the following July. Mark Tomas insisted that he had no intention of going to such a place. Thinking back on this, the idea was ridiculous. He was so out of control and non-compliant, no residential place would ever have considered him in the state he was in. In retrospect, Tim had to have been in some denial also. We were having emergency meetings weekly so no long-range plan was a logical answer to what was happening in the moment. His years seeing Mark Tomas weekly and the relationship they had built clouded his assessment of an escalating problem.

Things heated up as Mark began to have rage episodes at school. I was called to take him home for a five-day suspension. He was verbally abusive to the assistant principal and he had threatened her. He would threaten me in front of the school personnel and it was obvious that they were fearful for my wellbeing. When he was on suspension, I had to work. The plan was for Mark to stay at home and he had a list of various activities in which to occupy his time. He often left the house and was not home when I arrived at 3 pm. When he returned later in the evening, he would not disclose where he had been. There was one neighborhood in our town where he would hang out with some boys there, so if we were trying to find him, we would drive over there first. But if he was not there, we had no idea where he went when he traveled into Roxbury, a troubled area in the inner city.

He returned from suspension and within two weeks was suspended again. This time, Mark Tomas and some of his friends had physically assaulted another student. His final suspension was for threatening to kill the shop teacher. I was humiliated by his actions. They were the very antithesis of our values. He would become angry with me for not defending him in these meetings. How could I possible defend him when I found his behavior reprehensible? On one occasion, he did cry and blame everyone else, although he appeared to have an awareness of the futility of this approach. He said he did not know why he was doing these things. After his third suspension in three months, the school called an emergency meeting. In addition to Mark Tomas, Mark and I, his therapist Tim was also was invited to the meeting.

The school said they were not capable of handling him in the public-school system. They admitted that one male teacher reported that he feared for himself and his family. I could not but agree with their assessment. The suspensions were not accomplishing anything worthwhile and he was falling farther and farther behind in his schoolwork. A decision was made for him to attend an alternative school that worked with troubled children in a nearby town. We raised the issue of his need for a longer-term residential placement. Mark Tomas was devastated by this decision. He perceived it as a plan to try and separate him from his friends. He felt we had all turned against him. He did go for the interview at the alternative school. He was well-behaved during the interview and he was accepted into the program. He had no desire to attend this school, but he knew he had no other alternative.

Things at home were going no better. I would rush home from work each day in a frenzy to arrive before he did. I was afraid to leave him alone with his brother and sister. I was also afraid of his bringing his new 'friends' into our home.

The situation finally came to a head when I received a phone call at work from Andy. He was asking advice about a hypothetical situation of 'a boy who knows someone who is doing wrong things and was wondering if that boy should tell someone'. It was obvious who this hypothetical boy was and when I asked Andy to tell me the things that were bothering him, he became upset and tearful while on the phone. I rushed home and had a long agonizing talk with Andy. Mark Tomas was not home, so we had time to talk this through.

He told me, albeit reluctantly, that a seventeen-year-old boy arrived at the house in a car to talk to Mark Tomas. This boy was very angry and was demanding money that was owed to him. Mark Tomas got in the car with the boy and went to our bank and withdrew $50.00 from our account to pay the boy back. I had been sleeping with my pocketbook next to the bed, but apparently, this was not sufficient vigilance. Mark had stolen my debit card. His brother then told me that Mark had been doing drugs and was possibly dealing. He said Mark had smoked marijuana in front of him in the playroom and had, on one occasion, cajoled Andy into joining him. He said he was fearful of telling us about what was going on and worried that Mark Tomas would never forgive him. He was caught in an impossible situation.

He blamed himself for 'ratting' on his brother yet he knew things were out of hand and that we needed to know what was happening. My head was spinning, but I praised him for being courageous and letting me know what was happening. Another corner had been turned, this time with enormous complications. I was honest with Andy and did not try to sugarcoat the situation or spout platitudes such as: 'it will be all right'. I let him know that the decisions that had to be made were being made by his parents, not by him. I also reminded him that it was Mark's actions that had led us to this point. I stressed that Mark Tomas needed help and it was our job to get him the help that he needed.

I called Tim, the therapist, and he agreed that this needed to be dealt with right away. He also warned me that if Mark Tomas became violent, then we needed to call the police. I then called Mark at work, reported what had happened and he left work and come home. We talked together and waited for Mark Tomas to get home. When he did arrive, Andy and Beth were sent upstairs and told to stay in their rooms with the doors closed.

Our conversation started calmly, we told him what we had learned, and of course, it was clear that the information had come from his brother. At first, Mark Tomas tried to make up some unbelievable story to explain why he owed money. When it was clear that we were not buying this story, he lost control. We told him he was grounded and that our main task was to find some help for him as soon as possible. He started raging about his brother and threatening to kill him. Then he ran upstairs and began pounding on Andy's door. Both Andy and Beth were afraid of Mark Tomas when he was in this state. We rushed upstairs and told Mark Tomas to go down stairs and to leave his brother alone. He did come down, but then he would get enraged again and rush back upstairs.

Mark grabbed Mark Tomas to stop him; he raised his fist at him and then at me. While Mark was grabbing him to prevent his running back upstairs, they somehow landed on the floor together. Mark started complaining that his dad was hurting him. I ran to the phone, dialed 911, and explained the situation briefly and that we needed assistance. Mark was trying to hold Mark Tomas' down on the floor, but Mark Tomas became even more frantic after my call to 911. I tried to assist Mark in holding Mark Tomas down. Now he was trying to hit us. He succeeded in biting my thigh and punching his father in the arm. He squirmed out of our reach and ran out the door. The police arrived right away. They searched the front yard, but it was dark and we did not find Mark.

The police interviewed us and took a history or recent episodes of violence by Mark Tomas upon me. They strongly urged us to file a restraining order for Mark Tomas to refrain from any violence against his siblings or me. Again, I called Tim, and he said I should file the order. I left Mark to help calm Andy and Beth and went to the police station to file the emergency order. I ended up spending hours at the police station as they had difficulty finding a judge on call. Mark was home, calling whomever he could think of. He located Mark Tomas at the address of one of his less reputable friends. His mother said she was not comfortable returning him to us! Mark called the police station and relayed this news. The police took down the address and said they would pick him up later when everyone was asleep as there would a less likely chance of any problems. A judge was finally located, he issued the order, and I was allowed to go home.

I was very tired but unable to relax. We waited up for the police to call stating that they had picked up Mark Tomas. They called at 2 am stating that they were at the address, they had Mark Tomas in custody and were bringing him to the police station. We were advised to arrive at the police station at 8 am to bring Mark's clothes for court. When I arrived at the police station, an officer took me aside and warned me that he had filed a 51A report (child abuse) as Mark was making accusations. By law, they had to file the report. Since he did not believe the accusations, he down played it so I didn't really think much about what he said.

I was told to go to the district court from the police station that morning. There would be a hearing scheduled on the restraining order. Tim had also advised me to fill out a CHINS petition (Child In Need of Services) while I was at the courthouse. He said that while it did not have any real clout, it could help us document the need for placement in a residential program.

The next day will continue to live on as one of the most horrendous days of my life. I naively thought that I would go to court to fill out papers and would come home with Mark Tomas to plan where we were to go from here. I thought the restraining order might actually help contain him. I told Mark that it was all right for him to go to work, that I did not expect anything major to occur. I said I would call him when I finished at the courthouse and give him an update.

The court experience was a nightmare. I went to the clerk's office shortly after 8 am as I had been directed. I was told that I needed to wait until 8:45 to check in with them. At 8:45, I was told to wait until my name was called. I sat on a bench to wait and observed that the courthouse lobby was steadily filling up with people. Finally, my name was called and a man approached me. He said he was a prosecutor from the District Attorney's office and he needed to interview me. He took me to an office in the basement and began to ask me questions about incidents leading up to my filing a restraining order. He then told me that Mark and I were being investigated for child abuse. Mark Tomas had alleged that his father had physically assaulted him with a number of physical blows and that I had inflicted numerous cigarette burns on his arms.

He said two separate 51A affidavits had been filed and that child abuse petitions take precedence over restraining orders. For a few seconds, I was in shock. This just couldn't be happening. As the haze in my head started to clear, I totally lost my composure. I began sobbing and was unable to stop. I am usually a private person and I do not like to cry in front of people I know, let alone strangers. But I was totally unprepared for what was occurring. I felt like my head was exploding and I was afraid that I might faint. I was devastated that Mark Tomas could make these awful accusations about us. And telling people that I was torturing him, I just couldn't comprehend it.

Knowing that the accusations were false was little consolation. We now had to justify ourselves to the court officials for actions our son had fabricated. And I was hurt that Mark Tomas, in his anger, would think to hurt me this way.

Mark Tomas did have a series of scars on his arms that looked like cigarette burns. But they had been self-inflicted about six months prior to this. I confronted Mark Tomas when the wounds were new and he denied that they were cigarette burns. He said that he was picking at old cuts and that he had made them worse. While it was true that he was a picker and had always removed any scab from his cuts, it was clear to me that these wounds looked like cigarette burns.

I had asked him at the time, if he had done this as a form of self-destructive behavior and he denied this. Andy later told me that he had observed Mark burn a cigarette into his arm several times to prove he could withstand pain without making a sound.

The prosecutor seemed friendly and was concerned with my distraught state. He said he had to report to the District Attorney, who would make a recommendation to the judge. I learned then that the police had filed assault and battery charges against Mark Tomas based on their questioning me regarding past incidents with Mark for the emergency restraining order.

At this point, I didn't know whom I could trust. The whole situation had taken on a life of its own. The prosecutor said a female probation officer with a lot of experience had interviewed Mark Tomas and she believed his side of the story. I was advised to obtain the services of a lawyer to protect myself. He also said the Department of Welfare had been contacted and they would be involved behind the scenes and that they would have a say in any decision that was made.

I was finally able to get control of my emotions so that I could think about what I next needed to do. I called Mark and filled him in on what was occurring. He left work in Boston to join me at the courthouse later that morning.

The probation officer called me in for an interview. She was a short woman who emanated an aura of authority and had a no-nonsense manner of talking. My first impression of her was that she looked stern and that she seemed to be very angry with me. She started the interview by saying it was appalling that Mark Tomas was in lock-up in the basement of the courthouse. She reported that he looked sad and dejected, he had not been able to sleep the previous night, and he had not had any food since the previous afternoon. I thought she was implying that this was my fault. I was right—she was implying that this was all my fault.

She began asking me about Mark Tomas's scars. I explained what I knew about the scars and about the recent events leading up to our being in court. She was still reserved and skeptical and said she would confer with the social worker from the Department of Social Services (DSS). I was dismissed from her office and searched to find a pay phone and proceeded to call Mark Tomas's therapist. I shared the details of the morning and he reported that he knew the Probation Officer and he respected her. He said he would call her and try to get things back on track. Mark arrived while I was talking to Tim on the phone.

Next, a pleasant young woman from the District Attorney's office interviewed me. She seemed moved by my distress and stated she would keep me informed on the progress of events. I later learned that she was victims' rights advocate. This was a tedious, emotionally draining, long day. Since it was not a Tuesday, which was designated as juvenile day, there was no juvenile judge in the courthouse.

Since most judges do not like to hear juvenile cases, they tend to leave them till the end of the day after all other business has been taken care of. Periodically, we would ask how Mark Tomas was doing and we were repeatedly told that he was very angry with us. Mark and I agonized over whether we should just drop the restraining order and try and find another approach. We found out it was a moot point. The Hingham police had filed the assault and battery charge and we had no power to stop that.

As part of what seemed like an endless series of interviews, the Assistant D.A. met with us. She had reviewed the interviews done by her assistants and had met with Mark Tomas. Mark Tomas did not earn any points with her in the interview as he was angry and rude to her. She let us know that she took the Assault and Battery charge very seriously. And she felt an obligation to protect us in whatever way she could, and she was especially concerned with my safety. She said that this was a particularly messy case and that ultimately, the judge would decide. We were told we would not be called to the courtroom until all adult business was over.

Since we would have to wait until later afternoon, we asked if it would be possible to meet with Mark Tomas. She reluctantly agreed and he was brought up from lock-up to the probation visiting room. Our first reaction was one of relief that he looked physically all right. We sat down with him and he glowered at us. He became verbally abusive to me, at which point, the supervising court officer told him "Watch your language". Mark Tomas was verbally abusive to him in response to this warning. The court officer terminated the interview.

At long last, we were ushered into the courtroom for a closed hearing with the judge. The Assistant D.A. spoke first and was followed by Mark Tomas's court-appointed attorney. The judge asked me if the incidents listed in the assault and battery charge against Mark Tomas were accurate. I felt I had to be honest and said yes. Next, he asked Mark Tomas a few questions and Mark Tomas repeated the lie that we had abused him. It is impossible to describe what this felt like. Unless, you have been there, it is not possible to totally understand. Mark Tomas scowled at us and was flippant with the judge. That did not help his case.

The judge said that it was clear that a cooling-off period was indicated and the Department of Social Services needed to be consulted. We were convinced that placing Mark Tomas in a juvenile detention center would only make things worse, so we indicated that we were strongly against this option. Frantic calls were made by Mark to his mother in West Roxbury to see if she would agree to take Mark Tomas for the weekend with Mark's brothers, (who also lived in West Roxbury) checking in to make sure things were safe.

Mark's mother said that although she really did not understand what was going on, she would do anything to help. She and Mark's sister, Lisa, arrived at the courthouse by about 4:40PM. The Probation Officer verified that they were willing to take Mark Tomas and we went back in the courtroom. The judge ordered Mark Tomas to go home with them, and we were told to have no contact with him over the weekend. Mark's mother and sister were directed to drop him off at school on Monday morning. I was directed to pick him up from school and bring him home for us to meet with the DSS social worker conducting the child abuse investigation.

I had been the first person to arrive at the courthouse that morning, and Mark and I were the last to leave that day. They locked the doors behind us. There was little to say that night; we were exhausted. What had started out as an attempt to seek help for our family had turned into a complicated and much more serious situation. It felt like we had been written into a poorly scripted and unrealistic B movie. But it was real and it was our life. At this point, it was hard to imagine that things could get any worse, but we were to find out that more was in store for all of us.

Mark called West Roxbury over the weekend to see how our son was doing. The report was that he was quiet and compliant. His uncles made visits to the house and talked with him. They told him that they understood adolescence was a difficult time and they would listen if he wanted to talk with them. He was pleasant, but offered little. On Monday morning, his Aunt Lisa brought him to school. I picked him up and the DSS worker met us at the house. She talked with Mark and me first and then met with Mark Tomas. He admitted to her that we had not abused him and that he had made up the accusations because he was angry with us.

She set up a contract of ground rules for us. She met with us again one week later. Between visits, she contacted Mark Tomas's therapist, the Junior High School, the Alternative School, and our relatives. She told us that her recommendation would be that the child abuse complaint 'would not be substantiated'. We would receive a formal notice in writing after she reviewed the case with her supervisor. She told us we could now apply for voluntary services from her department. She stressed that Mark Tomas's Hispanic heritage played an important role in his search for identity and it affected the way other adolescents saw him as well.

We returned to court and the juvenile judge put Mark Tomas on probation, stipulating that he attend school and follow its rules, refrain from all acts or threats of violence at home and that he continued attending therapy. He was required to meet monthly with his Probation Officer for one year.

Mark Tomas said he did not like the alternative school he was attending, but he was behaving. The staff there did not see the behavior we were seeing at home. He was assigned the Probation Officer that we met the first time in court. Despite my initial encounter with her, she became our ally in setting limits and she supported our efforts to get him the services he needed. There were no more acts of violence, but there was little change in his attitude. He remained very angry with us and I suspected that this was only a temporary cease-fire. We remained at an impasse regarding his socializing with his friends. He said clearly he would continue to meet with his friends.

Our case was opened with the DSS and we were assigned a social worker to complete an assessment and make recommendations. Her name was Laura and she became a pivotal person in our lives. We were very fortunate to have her in our corner. She was thorough and competent. She was bright and personable. She conveyed a strength of purpose. She was able to make suggestions without appearing judgmental. She was sensitive and caring without becoming over-involved. I trusted her, which made this unavoidably intrusive process more bearable. Her recommendation after the assessment was that Mark Tomas was in need of residential placement. But making a recommendation and getting the state bureaucracy to implement this are two very different things.

Mark Tomas remained angry and miserable. He was unreachable and I worried that we were just biding time and not making any headway. He remained oppositional and made it clear that he felt he could do whatever he wanted without having to account to us. On two occasions, he stayed out all night. One of these times, a girl called at 11:30 pm to tell us that he was all right, but he would not be coming home. She would not tell us where he was.

We had been told the wait for residential placement could take months and I doubted that the situation would hold for that long a period of time. Mark Tomas began to resent his therapist. This relationship had been positive for years, but as Tim confronted him and tried to set ground rules for him to follow at home, Mark Tomas started to pull back from him. His anger at me grew stronger in his sessions with Tim, so much so that Tim called me on two occasions to warn me that I was in serious potential danger. This is known as a 'Tarasoff warning'. Therapists are required to implement this when someone in therapy discloses that they are having homicidal thoughts to harm a specific individual and the threat is credible and potentially doable.

He suggested that I hide any knives, hide our bankcards, and Mark Tomas's bankbook. He said he thought it likely that once he secured some money, he might run away and use the money in pursuit of a more dangerous lifestyle. I understood the dangerousness behind being notified of a Tarasoff warning by a mental health professional. And I knew that most of Mark Tomas's threats were directed at me. I do not think that Mark really believed things were really acutely dangerous. You can't convince someone who does not want to believe horrible events could occur. We did not share these warnings with Andy or Beth; they were in no danger and they did not need to be burdened with this.

It was so frustrating. No matter what we tried, all our dealings with Mark Tomas were negative. I felt burned out and drained. I had this horrible anxious feeling that I now carried around with me all the time. He was picking fights with his brother and sister. It was difficult for them to have their friends come over to our home. Several times, I had to put them in the car with their friends and drive the friends home as Mark was starting to escalate and become abusive to me. He was their older brother and he was being a pain.

It felt like we were being terrorized. When Mark Tomas became angry with me now, he had an ominous look on his face. I told his therapist that we could not go on living like this.

He agreed and said it was time to begin planning for an involuntary hospitalization. Tim was worried about Mark Tomas's potential for violence, particularly when confronted with having to seek treatment away from home. For the next three weeks, we went back and forth about how to coordinate such an effort. He did not feel it was wise to have a showdown with Mark Tomas at his office.

He contacted the alternative school and they had no desire to have this occur at their school since the police would invariably be involved. Tim thought it likely that the police should be present since Mark would be very angry. No plan we discussed could be implemented smoothly. And none of this had to happen if services had been available when we needed them. It had been agreed by the DSS that Mark needed residential placement over three months prior. And no one could give us any idea when a residential placement would open up for Mark. We were expected to survive indefinitely in the untenable state of limbo. It made no sense.

We were now reaching the finale. I came home from work and went up to my room to change my clothes. On my bed, I found a large meat cleaver. My bureau had several knife slashes through the top surface. Even more frightening was when I again faced the bed; I noticed that my pillow had a number of knife gashes in it. The message was clear to me. If we did not take immediate action, I would be in danger.

And that had implications for the entire family, including Mark Tomas. I called Mark at work and asked him to come home. I called Tim, told him what I had found, and said that it was time to take action. We could wait no longer. He told me to bring Mark Tomas to his office with Mark once Mark got home. Mark arrived home and shortly thereafter, Mark Tomas arrived. We told him we had an emergency meeting with Tim. He sensed that something was up and said he was not going. We told him that he had no choice. I remember trying to pry his fingers off the doorknob as he initially tried to resist going out the door. He did get in the car and we drove to the therapist's office.

When we arrived, Tim was there with John, who was a co-therapist for the boys' group. They met with Mark Tomas alone. They discussed their concerns that things were out of control and they tried to get him to agree with a voluntary hospitalization on a child/adolescent psychiatric unit. He was against the idea.

Then John stayed in the room with Mark Tomas and Tim came out to talk to Mark and me in the waiting room. Since I was the Program Director of the Crisis Team, it meant that I not only understood the process involved in getting a child or an adult hospitalized, but I used that knowledge to train new clinicians who we hired. I was the clinical backup that was called during the night to have cases presented by clinicians who were doing evaluations and needed my authorization to either let someone return home with an out-patient follow-up or to make the determination that a person was not safe to return home and needed to be hospitalized. Here, in this situation, I wanted to be just a mother, but Tim had little experience with involuntary hospitalization. So, I had to walk him through the process, step by step.

He called a psychiatric hospital in a community twenty miles away that had a child and adolescent unit. They agreed to take him, but since it was after 5 pm, it was not possible to obtain insurance verification. The hospital stated that they would do that in the morning. Tim filled out the 'Commitment Paper', which in Massachusetts is referred to as a 'Section 12'. Then the police and the local ambulance were called. The police arrived first. At this point, Mark Tomas was told he would be going to the hospital. He was angry and surly, but he did not lose control. The ambulance arrived about twenty minutes later. Mark was belligerent getting on the stretcher, but he did comply. I rode with him in the ambulance and his father followed in our car.

As I rode in the ambulance, I reflected on the path that led to that moment and I clung to the hope that this sad conclusion would lead to us moving down a road that was less painful.

Many times, I have reflected back on that day. I wondered if I had over-reacted. Maybe the symbolism of the meat cleaver was just that—a symbol. Would other parents have handled the situation differently? I do not scare easily and I had been living day to day with fear and dread that something awful was coming. I felt that if my fears were correct and we didn't act, and he succeeded in trying to kill me, how could he and the rest of the family survive without tremendous repercussions?

Chapter 12
The Aftermath

Mark Tomas had been psychiatrically hospitalized. I thought that this could be the end of a bad time—a time when we had felt powerless as things spun out of control. I told myself: "Now, things will start to get back on track". Partly, this was a justification for pushing for the hospitalization and partly, it was wishful thinking. From the very beginning of the admission process, I began to have misgivings. From those initial misgivings, I came to be frustrated, then angry and disappointed.

Admitting your child to a psychiatric facility is a somewhat frightening experience. First of all, you are feeling tremendous guilt that you have handled things so badly that it has resulted in this 'last ditch effort'. Then, you are harboring an unrealistic hope that in resorting to hospitalization, you have ensured that things will get better. Your assumption (or at least my assumption) was that the expertise available in the hospital would, of course, accomplish what other resources you have tried and had been unable to do.

The admission process did nothing to reassure us that we had made the right decision. Mark Tomas was separated from us as soon as we entered the adolescent unit. Mark and I were escorted to a small interview room and a nurse joined us. The nurse interviewing us was pleasant, but she was unable to answer any of our questions about the unit procedures and treatment. She did not normally work on this unit and knew next to nothing about it, not even the basics. I asked her: "What was the unit routine? How would our son spend his day? What were the visiting hours? Were there family meetings?" She left the room to get a brochure about the unit and returned to say she could not find one. As this was a Friday night, she advised us to call Monday morning to find out who his physician and social worker would be. We left feeling Mark Tomas was at least safe, but we were otherwise not reassured.

The inability to get information about what was happening proved to be a consistent theme during the course of his staying there. That first weekend, we called the adolescent unit each day to find out how Mark Tomas was doing. The responses were vague: "He is fine". When we pressed for details, no one was able to tell us. We were directed to speak with his doctor and caseworker. On Monday, we started making phone calls to the people assigned to him and our phone calls most often were never returned. We left message after message asking that someone contact us. The one phone call that was returned resulted in our intake assessment interview with his doctor and case manager, which took place at the end of his first week in the hospital.

They took a history of our observations of Mark Tomas's problems and behaviors. We told them we believed that underneath all of his anger, we felt that he was depressed and very unhappy. I spoke of the years of therapy, his learning difficulties, his acting out, and his escalating behaviors as well as the various medication trials. I spoke of my strong feeling, that at least some of his rage was related to his adoption and his transracial identity. I also mentioned his substance abuse and our real fears for our safety over the past six months. We shared how the family was impacted by his behavior—how it had affected Andy and Beth and how it had affected us his parents.

We were honest in sharing that we had gone from sad to depressed and now were experiencing a sense of futility. We shared our fears that our family was unraveling under all the stress. We told them that this step to having Mark Tomas hospitalized was our recognition that we had tried everything we could think of and had met with no success—and that this was the turning point for us.

We had made a decision that he could not return home until he received treatment for his difficulties and that we had some indication that things had improved. We gave the names and phone numbers of all the agencies and individuals we had already been involved with and asked them to contact these people to verify what we were saying. We let them know that a recommendation for residential placement had already been made and informed them of the problems in implementing the recommendation due to several bureaucracies having to be involved for the three agency cost share agreements before a placement could be found.

We were asked what we wanted to happen during Mark's hospitalization. We asked that he receive an extensive evaluation leading to a diagnosis and that treatment be initiated for his current problems. We were assured that he would receive such an evaluation, he would have daily meetings with his doctor and case manager, psychological testing would be done, family meetings would be held and his medication would be reviewed, etc. We left the meeting reassured and hopeful. We felt listened to! That was short-lived and we became increasingly dissatisfied. No one ever met with us again, there was no family meeting—that one intake meeting was our only face-to-face contact with the doctor and social worker!

Visiting Mark Tomas at the hospital was a painful experience. He was enraged with us for putting him there. He was hostile, sullen, and unforthcoming with any information about what was happening at the hospital. He said that he was so angry with us that he would tell the hospital people whatever they wanted to hear so that he would be discharged and that when he returned home, we would pay for his ordeal. On one visit, he threatened to kill us when he returned home. We reported these incidents to the staff on the unit and they said that they would inform his doctor. We requested supervised visits and we were urged to stay away and give him time to cool off.

I was depleted and anxious. Mark and I talked and we agreed that I needed a rest. I made plans to visit my good friend Debbie who now resided in Ohio. I needed a neutral place to relax and restore myself for what I knew to be the struggles ahead.

When I called Mark Tomas to let him know that I would be gone for a few days, his response was to say: "Mom, it isn't helpful for you to run away from your problems!"

So, off to Ohio I went. Mark's family did not understand my need to get away. I felt badly that they did not understand, but I went away anyway. I knew that if I did not do something to take care of myself, I was going to be useless to everyone. And I needed some distance from my family problems so I could muster up the strength to continue dealing with them. We had a long road ahead of us, which included the ongoing struggle of fighting the system to get Mark Tomas the help he deserved.

It was so great to see Debbie; she was just what I needed. I was blessed to have her as a friend. The five days sped by and they were indeed restorative. But they were not carefree. While I was there, Mark called to tell me that Mark Tomas's case manager had called him to tell him that Mark Tomas needed to be discharged home the following day since the insurance company had refused payment. After much discussion, we decided to stand firm and to tell the hospital we would not take him home.

We were upset and now angry. Mark Tomas had been hospitalized for over two weeks and no attempt had been made to inform us about his progress, no sharing of his doctor's impressions, his recommendations, etc. Mark had actually kept count and we had made twenty-one calls to either the doctor or the case manager that met with no response whatsoever. We had not gone through this ordeal just to find ourselves in the same situation two weeks later.

We were anxious about the position we were taking, but we were going to get help for our son come 'hell or high water'. When Mark called the hospital case manager to let them know we would not take our son home, he went on to tell them how unhappy we were with their services so far. We did not know how they expected us to take our son home when he was unable to tolerate being in our presence for over five minutes. The staff had suggested we restrict our contact with him and visit less yet now they were saying to take him home. It made no sense.

It turned out the issue was financial. The insurance company had refused to pay based on the clinical information the hospital gave to the insurance company. The doctor's position was that Mark Tomas suffered from a 'character disorder' and that this was a family problem and did not warrant hospital level of care. A 'character disorder' is not considered an acute condition. It is classified as a personality disorder, and the specific personality disorder to which the doctor was referring was antisocial. That diagnosis involves characteristics of having little conscience and results in acting with no regard to others or to society at large. It is not allowed to be used in children at all. It is considered long-standing in nature and cannot effectively be treated with medication. In fact, it does not have a favorable prognosis. Mark Tomas was acting out in very exaggerated proportions with no regard for others. We still believed that he regretted his behavior despite all his rage. We were told that his substance abuse was more extensive than we had been aware of previously.

Both the substance abuse and the rage led to the acting out without regard for others or of the ultimate consequences. Combine these factors with adolescent rebellion then adding problems of identity complicated by adoption issues that were transracial. And it should be clear that a diagnosis of an adolescent personality disorder is much too simplistic. The hospital only looked at his behaviors—they never even peeked under the surface. The doctor by giving his impression to the insurance company was further complicating our ability to find resources for our son. I suspect that Mark Tomas must have really gotten under this doctor's skin for the doctor to have given him that diagnosis, knowing it was a violation of pediatric psychiatric practice.

And the hospital felt that this was a 'family problem'. Of course, it was a family problem. He was a teenager living in a family; his actions effected everyone else the same way that our actions affected him. We had owned that we had a family problem, we even owned that we were unable to fix it on our own—that was why we had sought out their help. We had asked for family meetings; they never held even one as part of his treatment at the hospital. His medication regime was not changed. We asked for and were told that Mark would have psychological testing. I requested a copy of the testing—I was dumbfounded. I was given a handwritten in pencil one-page copy that would not have met any standard for a first-year psychology trainee. It was so sub-standard that it could not be used in any packet of information that residential programs might request. (A year later, his psychiatrist at the hospital made the news as he was convicted of inappropriate sexual contact with male child patients and he lost his license to practice medicine and went to jail.)

From my perspective, this was an example of one of the limitations in the treatment of children. As the system moved to a managed care model of mental health, children became particularly vulnerable to weaknesses within the health system. Sure, managed care was a response to past abuses by service providers but managed care had not done enough and had shown a disheartening lack of commitment by society to care for and protect its children. Often, they have been written off as over-stimulated teenagers instead of providing valuable intervention. Not providing positive interventions in a timely manner can spell the difference between a teen that can be helped to become a productive member of society and a teen who is siphoned off from the normal social flow to juvenile detention and a series of later incarcerations.

Giving a teen the diagnosis of character disorder is one step down that path to potential adult institutionalization. It flags the child to other therapists and child service agencies as a difficult case who may not be worth the effort. Since funding for child programs is inadequate, obtaining help for your child is further complicated by turf battles between different child agencies. Each agency tries to protect its limited resources by stating a referral for services is the domain of another agency, not theirs.

After we refused to take Mark Tomas home, we became a problem for the hospital. Their already spotty communication with us became non-existent. We obtained our information second-hand for the various agencies they contacted. A residential placement was the needed disposition, but that proved impossible to arrange in a timely fashion. There was an enormous amount of red tape that had to be gone through in order to secure such a placement, so an interim placement had to be found as a way station.

Securing a residential placement for your child is a cumbersome process. Unless you are very wealthy, the cost is prohibitive. Most placements are funded by state agencies Department of Social Services (DSS), Department of Mental Health (DMH), Division of Youth Services (DYS), Department of Education, (DOE). In our case, months before at a CORE evaluation for Mark, it was agreed that DSS and the local school system would cost-share a residential placement for him. We learned now that the agreement was tentative. No contract had been signed and there was no mechanism to move it along in a hurry. DSS had a number of bureaucratic steps to be gone through to move a contractual agreement from the local level to the head of the state agency.

In order to secure an interim placement, we had to involve a third agency—the Department of Mental Health. I applied for voluntary services and he was initially rejected based on the hospital's diagnosis of 'character disorder'. Eventually, the DMH agreed to provide short-term services for Mark Tomas. This short-term placement was being done to give DSS additional time to come up with a longer-term residence. They agreed to fund Mark Tomas in one of their adolescent acute residential treatment programs for a period of time not to exceed sixty days. But there was no vacancy at that program at this point in time. The local community mental health center had a Crisis Team component, which included an adolescent Respite House. They were contacted to interview Mark Tomas at the hospital to determine if he was appropriate for this facility.

At this point, things became sticky. I was the Program Director of this Crisis Team. Issues of confidentiality and favored treatment or denial of treatment now had to be considered, dealt with, and resolved. It was decided that as a resident of the area, my family was entitled to the same mental health services as any other resident—regardless of the fact that I was an employee of the agency.

Securing the Respite House placement took two interviews. On the first interview, a child specialist of the crisis team and the DMH Case Manager assigned to Mark Tomas did the screening. Mark was provocative and played to the fullest his 'I'm my bad self' persona. He would not clearly agree to the rules and reported to them that he was in possession of a gun! They initially said that they did not feel they would be able to manage him. The hospital insisted he be moved to a detention center and all the agencies involved, including his Probation Officer, felt this was not in his best interest. The Probation Officer was adamant in telling the hospital it was a terrible plan.

She stated he would receive no real treatment there. He would be exposed to a negative environment, which would only make his problems worse and she refused to agree with the plan. It again looked like the only option was the interim Respite House. He was interviewed a second time. The hospital felt Mark had sabotaged the first interview thinking if they said no, he would be able to come home. By now, Mark Tomas had been in the hospital for three weeks. On the second interview, he was much more reasonable, agreed to follow the rules, and said that he did not have possession of a gun.

The hospital experience was a negative one for Mark Tomas and for us, his parents. To their credit, they kept him safe at a time when we needed emergency intervention. They were saddled with a difficult situation. If he had been psychotic, then he would have been given medication, probably he would have responded positively, and he could have returned home. But he did not suffer from a psychotic disorder; he had a myriad of problems that needed attention and would not have a quick solution. He was also very resistant to facing these problems as they were so painful to him.

The hospital saw its role as providing acute care and felt these problems were beyond their scope. On some level, I could understand this. What I had a difficult time coming to terms with was that I felt we were treated very badly. As parents, we were suffering terribly from this ordeal and there was no attempt to reach out to us; we received no support. There was no sense of working together to find any solutions to the problems we were facing. They, by their treatment of us, created more stress at a time when we were at our lowest point. We also felt that they never scratched below the surface in their assessment of our son. They housed him and kept him safe, and for that, we were grateful. But that was all we were grateful for. They made finding residential placement more difficult than it already had become.

The Respite House stay was uneventful. Mark was very well-behaved and there was no problem. The house manager was a caring, older woman who treated us with respect and gave us updates whenever we called. On weekends, Mark Tomas was able to come home and spend the day. He was less overtly angry. I think that it had finally dawned on him that he would not be coming home with us and that his future was uncertain.

Behind the scene, the time was spent planning the next placement. Mark went on an interview with his DMH case manager to the Acute Residential Treatment center and he was accepted for this program. He had been lonely at the Respite House as he was the only child there at that time. He was looking forward to being with other teenagers again. Initially, he did very well and we were getting positive reports. After about six weeks, the honeymoon was over and he began getting in trouble. He was caught with drugs brought back by one of the other boys in the program. He denied any· responsibility, but we learned from Andy that he had, in fact, brought the drugs to our home and showed them to Andy.

Other residents of the program accused Mark and this other boy of giving drugs to other residents in the program. By the end of his stay there, the staff changed their initial thoughts and told us that they agreed with our assessment that he needed a longer-term placement. They felt he had leadership potential, that he had an influence on others, and that this skill needed to be channeled in a more constructive direction. This program was meant to be a six-week assessment and then most of the children returned to their homes. It was known from the onset that this would not be the case with him. But at the end of six weeks, there was no DSS placement in sight.

I contacted the placement that had been mentioned as a possible fit and arranged for an interview without DSS sanction. I sent our own packet of information about Mark Tomas to this program. Mark Tomas went on the interview with Mark and me; this time, he made a good impression. The interviewer had a no-nonsense approach and she was very clear in discussing the reality of the program as well as Mark Tomas's warranting such a hard-nosed approach. After my initial jarring reaction, I realized I found her refreshing. She was blunt but honest. She didn't try to gloss over the rules and the structure. She was seasoned and she conveyed the idea that the program could not be conned. To my surprise, Mark Tomas was taken aback only briefly. He too seemed refreshed by the raw and honest approach. Mark and I returned Mark Tomas to the ART and when we talked about this program, it was with a hopefulness we hadn't felt in a long time.

To our dismay, the next delay was brought on by turf battles of the three agencies involved. Instead of bogging you down with the details of that battle, I'll just stay that it became a stalemate. It was a tense time and we tried to stay out of the fray when different agencies were fighting with each other. But we were again in the place where Mark Tomas was expected to move on and there was nowhere for him to go. We were so frustrated with the bureaucracy and its lumbering, one-step-ahead-and-two-steps-back method of doing things. We were careful not to personalize it. The budget freeze within DSS was not one of our social worker's doing. It became time to take things into our own hands again.

Mark's family had repeatedly asked if they could help in any way. Now we needed their assistance. Two of Mark's brothers were close friends with a Massachusetts State Representative. They had met him through their mutual extracurricular activities as football referees on weekends. He had long served as a public official and was a committed and caring person who fought for human services for the people in his state. One of Mark's brothers contacted this legislator and explained our plight. He requested that we write a letter to him explaining the situation so he could determine if there was anything he could do to help us.

I had already warned our DSS worker that we were taking steps to move the system. We learned from her that while the freeze was in effect, no child could be placed in a DSS residential program. And since Mark could no longer stay where he was, DSS was looking into moving him to yet another ninety-day interim placement until the funding issue could be resolved. We were adamant that Mark Tomas was not going to be moved a fourth time in as many months—and to a program that was not geared to treating his problems.

I knew the system well enough to know that you have to go to the top to get decisions made and then they filter down the system. I told her I was writing a letter to people in the central administration who I felt had the power to make decisions. I was bypassing the regular chain of command and would be making waves. The letter detailing our difficulty obtaining residential placement was sent to the Commissioner of DSS and the Area Director. This was also the letter we forwarded to our contact in the legislature. The representative's secretary called me several times to clarify points so that they understood the problem clearly.

This representative scheduled a brief meeting with the Commissioner of DSS, gave her a letter he had written about our plight, and personally expressed his hopes that she could find a way to help us. He then asked us to wait a few days. Within forty-eight hours, we were notified that Mark Tomas's funding for residential placement had been granted by the Area Office of DSS! We felt we would be forever indebted to this wonderful man whose caring soul was willing to go to bat for our son.

We had finally reached the point we had been trying to reach for most of the last year. Help was in sight and it gave us renewed hope.

Looking for help was at times very fatiguing. It required maintaining focus, keeping the end in sight, and settling down for the long haul. There was one setback after another. During setbacks, it was important to keep the end result in mind. And it was very important to keep in mind every person along the way who tried to help in whatever way they could. The bureaucracy was a cold, huge machine, but it is made up of individuals who, when they become involved, do care. Neil, our DMH Case Manager was helpful and caring as well as understanding of our situation.

He bent over backwards whenever the opportunity presented itself. Laura, our DSS social worker was tireless as well as caring. Chris, the Probation Officer was supportive and fought for appropriate services for Mark. Tim, Mark's therapist stuck by us for years and was committed to Mark. Dr. Richard Netsky, Mark's outpatient psychiatrist was supportive and gentle in his approach of letting me know there was only so much we could do as the situation worsened. He gently pointed out to me that the family was floundering under the stress of Mark's escalation and that other alternatives needed to be searched for and obtained. Jane, the house manager of the Respite House was kind, open, and non-judgmental. The staff of the adolescent ART was caring, committed individuals.

They were the under-belly of the bureaucracy and they were all good caring people. They are what made the system work and they brought out the best in what the system had to offer. The uncaring part was the nameless system as a whole. The machine knew no names only numbers. It fights turf battles with agencies within its domain. To have change occur, you need to work with the people on the front lines and support them while you are fighting the larger battle with the system as a whole.

I know it is wrong for parents to have to go through such a struggle to get services for their child. I did not know how to change it. But I learned to get around it. I had a knowledge, because of my job, of how the system works. And that proved fortuitous for our child. But what about parents who do not know how to fight the system to get services for their child? Their child deserves services just as much as mine did. What do they do? I suspect some children languish without receiving the help they deserve. Without the needed help, many of their problems will undoubtedly worsen. Society as a whole plays a part in those children lives, because the system reflects our values, priorities, and our concern. It is inexcusable.

Chapter 13
1995 – 1996: The Program

On May 24, 1995, we brought Mark Tomas to the Institute for Family Life and Learning (IFLL) for admission to the program. He was now in a long-term placement. He was officially separated from us. It was an emotional experience that was becoming familiar, but I remained calm and collected. I knew with conviction that we were doing the right thing, but that did not make it any easier. We were now distanced physically and it stuck me then that much of what had gone on and had led to this point. I wondered if, on some unconscious level, this was Mark Tomas' way to show us how very distant he felt from us when we were a family together. We said our goodbyes in a reserved way, none of us wanting to breakdown. The program was an hour away and I cried all the way home.

It had been explained to us that for the first six weeks, Mark would not be able to come home. He needed a period of adjustment to settle in and the family needed a time of rest. For the first two weeks, there was to be no contact. We could and did check in with the staff regularly on how he was doing and to send messages to him that we loved him and thought about him every day. After two weeks, Mark and I were able to visit him at the program for a weekend afternoon. It did not go well. Our expectations were too high; we were so anxious to see him and make contact. Mark Tomas was unable to make light conversation and unwilling to describe his life there in any detail. The visit deteriorated into his first expressing his resentment for our placing him there, followed by his becoming angry with us, and then his silence.

When we tried to reengage him, he became verbally abusive and we left in less than an hour. The next weekend, we tried again. When he became hostile, we sought out a staff person and asked him to sit with us and attempt to mediate. Again, we had to leave after a short time. The third weekend, the visit was cancelled due to his behavior on the previous visits. If things had gone well, we would have been at the point where we would have been able to take him off the ground for a few hours. The fourth weekend, the visit went better. He was able to remain calm. Mark Tomas had been there for a month and was finally beginning to settle in. He was still cocky, and with the exception of one major blow up, there had been little acting up by Mark in the program. The staff thought he was adjusting well.

We had our first parents' orientation meeting and that was helpful. Just being in a room with people who were going through the same experience was comforting. We shared our experiences and our fears and asked questions about the program. For the first time in a long time, we didn't feel alone. Every Tuesday evening, a parents meeting was held. The format differed from week to week. Some weeks, we shared concerns with each other and other times, we shared how weekends home were going.

Sometimes, it was didactic and one of the clinicians would discuss a particular topic such as substance abuse, the philosophy of the program, setting limits, etc. The second and third Tuesday of the month was allocated to multi-family group. I loved these meetings. This included a large group of boys from the House 1 (where Mark was a resident) and their parents. It did not include boys whose parents were not in attendance. It was run informally and the boys sat in an inner circle and the parents sat in the outer circle.

Discussions would center on what was occurring in the House with the residents explaining the philosophy and sharing the rules and routine of the program. We also talked about weekends home. These groups were powerful. You had the benefit of witnessing the interaction between the residents with each other, giving each other feedback. Parents were questioning children who were not their own about their actions, questioning why they said or did something and giving their feedback to that particular child. It was a way of communicating indirectly with Mark Tomas at a time when he was not willing or able to talk to us on his own. I felt comfortable in the group and became involved before either Mark or Mark Tomas began to speak. I developed a real affection for some of the boys and their parents. There was a bond of having gone through hell together. And it was amazing to see the adolescents take constructive criticism from another parent in the group when that boy could not tolerate this from his own parent. It was also reaffirming. I started gaining back some of my self-confidence as a parent.

On the fourth Tuesday of the month, the parents group met in House 1. This was experiential. We would observe the residents and staff conduct house meetings, have confrontations, evaluate each other's performance, and give each other feedback. The parents were encouraged to participate and give feedback of our observations and ask questions when we did not understand a particular interaction.

The best way for me to describe the program was that it was an 'emotional boot camp'. It was very structured, had lots of rules, and had clear expectations for behavior with clear consequences, which were consistently metered out. It was tough but caring. It was a program for acting-out kids and it was the end of the line for many of them. If they didn't make it here, there was a high likelihood for a majority of the kids would end up in detention centers or jail. The focus of the program was in learning to express your feelings directly rather than acting them out.

The goal was to reprogram a group of kids who had already become fixated on acting out without thinking through the consequences on themselves and others. Behaviors were dealt with immediately and there was no room for exception based on mitigating factors. The mission was to provide these teens the opportunity to learn new skills to be able to survive and be successful within society. They were training kids to delay impulses and how to say what you mean in a way that someone could hear it. There was a lot of emphasis on the part substance abuse played into the behaviors they had exhibited that brought them to the program. They assisted the teenagers in exploring why that had turned to alcohol, drugs, and violence.

Side by side with all the rules were large amounts of positive feedback for each step that was done well. If you bought into their system and trusted them, the program could serve you well. A lot of the adolescents they accepted were already so far down their destructive path that they did not have the capacity to trust and those kids did not make it here. The staff would say this as a matter of fact and it scared me. This was our last hope and I was desperate for it to work for our son.

Five weeks had passed and we were able to take Mark Tomas out for a few hours. We planned a non-threatening activity. We went to a movie and then stopped to get something to eat. There were no problems; we had one successful outing off the grounds. The next weekend came and we went to a local mall. Mark Tomas got angry briefly over his wanting us to buy him a baseball cap, but he was able to turn his attitude around quickly. We might have bought it for him if he hadn't demanded it, but we said no. We didn't want to have a sour taste in our mouths that the visit went well because we had bought him off. And the demand to buy it for him smacked of familiar behavior. He had been able to put it aside, a big step for him.

We had the six-week assessment meeting and Mark was now scheduled to begin weekend visits home. The treatment plan included: anger management, substance abuse treatment, identity issues focusing on adoption and cross-cultural themes, school performance, and family therapy. The house had groups for most of these issues and in addition, he met weekly with a therapist. His treatment team consisted of a teacher from the program's school, his clinician, and a mental health counselor from his house.

The team reviewed weekly reports from house and school staff on progress, reviewed his weekend report, which we were required to fill out. The team made decisions about his privileges, altered his treatment goals, and coordinated his needs within the program. After about eight weeks into the program, we began weekends home. The first few visits home, a counselor from House 1 drove him home and reviewed expectations before he left. Mark would drive him back on Sunday afternoons. After the first few weekends, we did both pick up and return.

We fell into a routine. We called them and met with them to give and receive feedback. Any problems or rough spots we reported so that we could all be working together. Mark

Tomas's house counselor, Mike, was a major support to us. We trusted him. He was able to balance our concerns and Mark Tomas's with a style that was comfortable to all of us. It was evident that he liked Mark and we felt Mark was in good hands. Mark Tomas began to invest in the program and was a star there.

When he began learning new ways to communicate his feelings to us, he would get emphatic and dogged in trying to convince me of a point he was trying to make. I would begin to get uneasy and feel that I was being pressured or bullied into agreeing with him. He had moved from physically acting out to exerting verbal pressure. It was a step in the right direction, but it still had residual overtones for the past. We were able to talk about it and in family therapy, set up some ground rules for discussions. He needed to respect my stating I needed him to back off when I felt a discussion was going nowhere. We had to realize that there would be times when we had to agree to disagree on a point and table it for later discussion.

Getting to this point was not easy. There were times we would have flare-ups where the arguments got heated. There were a few times when we thought about taking him back to the program early. And there were times when he felt totally misunderstood. He would get frustrated, then angry, and dissolve in tears. In general, it was on Sunday when things erupted. It was the day he had to return to the program. Feelings that built up over the weekend spilled out in a rush on Sundays. All of us had less reserves for dealing with powerful emotional issues. The main issue for me was the expression of anger and being able to tolerate it at acceptable levels. For his father, it was feeling that he was respected and listened to.

Mark Tomas and his father began to try and establish better ways of communicating and this freed me up. I had been the go-between them for years and it had not proved satisfactory to any of us. I was more than willing to step back and let Mark step up. As their relationship improved, there was less tension between Mark and me. I had been resentful of being the go-between. I had received both of their negative comments about one another. I went from one brushfire to another and I learned not to show anger as there was enough going around to fuel a nuclear power station.

Now things were beginning to feel considerably better. But I was clearly able to state that I needed to feel unthreatened and that was my focus for things being demonstrably better. The program staff began to talk about Mark Tomas's return home. I began to look forward to that after things began going better on weekend visits. In two therapy sessions, Mark Tomas formally made amends for things he had done and was specific in recounting them and the hurt that they had caused to each of us. Forgiving him was easy, but forgetting would take longer.

Mark Tomas's progress in the program moved him up in the hierarchy from Younger Peer, to Older Peer, to Expediter to Overseer. He had done so well that he was functioning in a quasi-staff role. The staff had him mentoring newer residents. This improved his self-esteem and deepened his relationships with the staff. The down side was that it lessened his relationship with his peers. Each step up gave him more responsibility and moved him away from them. By the time he became Overseer, he was beginning to feel pressured. He was unable to relax with the other residents when he had free time.

When they engaged in negative behaviors, it was hard for him to deal with them in his role as Overseer. He had grown as much as he could in House 1 and the decision was made to have him move to House 3. I had mixed feelings about this move at a time when he was nearing the point of returning home. I felt that if he was doing well, why upset the applecart. He was projected to return home in the coming months. His counselor, Mike explained to me that House 3 was a transition house for adolescents who would be leaving the program to live on their own.

It was a testing ground to see if Mark Tomas had internalized the gains he had made in House 1 and was able to apply them on his own. House 3 was much more loosely structured. The expectation was on the resident taking responsibility to follow the program with a minimum of direction. Mark Tomas would have to balance school, therapy groups, and work. He was expected to save 75% of his earnings and show he could delay his impulses to spend money indiscriminately. He would have more free time off the grounds. He would be given the opportunity to face temptation and apply the decision-making skills he had been taught. (More about this later.)

So, in the spring, Mark Tomas made the move to House 3 and was another step closer to returning home. After a few weeks of feeling like he was at loose ends and missing the camaraderie of his friends and staff in House 1, he settled in. He made friends with his roommate and enjoyed his newfound freedom. He got a job at a Taco Bell in a nearby mall and was proud of earning his paycheck. He spent free time 'chilling out' with his new friend, Tito. He told us that House 1 had a number of new residents and it was sometimes chaotic there, so he was glad to be in House 3 where things were less intense and he had more free time.

Then, it was May and things seemed to speed up. We were all a little nervous. We were all apprehensive as the time was approaching. Weekends home seemed a little edgy. We talked about setting up a structure that did not leave Mark Tomas with too much free time. It was hard to hear Mark Tomas express his misgivings about returning home. I tried to put it in the context of normal fears, general adolescent issues, and leaving behind a year that had been meaningful in his life. And truth be told, much as he cared for us, he did feel different from us. No amount of love could change that. We couldn't help being white middle-class parents any more than he could change being Hispanic.

My hope then was that as the years went on and he became an adult, he would be able to accept his reality, come to terms with it, and find a ground to stand on where his two worlds came together.

Chapter 14
1996: The Search

When we were in the process of applying for adoption, we had some discussion with the adoption worker regarding an adoptive child's desire to find his/her birth parents. The thinking sixteen years back when we had this discussion was children had enough to deal with in adolescence finding their identity without complicating the task. We were instructed to recognize the need to want to know about a family of origin and we should approach this by saying that we would help our child in any way we could, if they wanted information, when they reached their eighteenth birthday. At the time, we bought this logic. Our experience had shown what a faulty premise this was.

Mark Tomas' ability to attach to us, his behaviors, and the reality of his Hispanic heritage were all clear indicators, in retrospect, that identity issues for him could not be resolved without some connection with his roots.

I had learned that his very silence on the issue meant that the issue was so important and uncomfortable that he was unable to talk about it or deal with it in a direct fashion. How had we expected him to work out a comfortable identity for himself when he was so uncomfortable with the issue that all he could admit was that he was different. And he felt like he did not fit in, not with our white family, not with his white suburban friends, not with his white middle-class community. So, he developed the persona of the stereotypical misfit! That was how he had handled his budding adolescent identity. Because he had no pieces to fill in that connected him with his cultural heritage, he was unable to form a cohesive blending of his biological roots and his adoptive upbringing.

I am going back in time a few years here to share my education on the issues involved in transracial adoption and attachment. The first real recognition that I was on the right track came too late to avoid the path he had already embarked upon. Mark was in the eighth grade at the Junior High and we were already in crisis at home and Mark's anger was spilling over at school. He was already spending several hours a day in the special needs classroom (the Resource Room) and he resented it. It was another reminder that he was different from his peers. My first lesson came in the form of a phone call to Corinne Rayburn, at the suggestion of the Junior High Guidance Counselor.

Corrine was well-known in adoptive circles for her expertise with issues of adoption. The call was pivotal in focusing our energies on Mark's adoptive crisis. She asked me questions over the phone to get a sense of the severity of the problem. Having determined that, she reeled off statistical information regarding adoption attachment problems. I did not retain the actual statistics, but I did retain their significance. These statistics spoke to the fact that there was a growing body of knowledge that was coming to light, especially in adolescent children, around crisis of identity and attachment. Her first message to me was to reassure me that the problem was not the result of faulty parenting.

She did fault a lack of knowledge around the dynamics of the adoptive experience for the adoptee and the lack of education and advice given to adoptive parents when they are at the beginning of the adoptive process. I mentioned the behaviors Mark Tomas had been exhibiting. She related that they were consistent with a pattern of behaviors that were being seen by adoption specialists and was referred to as 'male adoptee rage'. As this had only recently been recognized, they were still trying to explain the underlying cause. Was there a genetic component that explained this? She did not know. But what we were living with was real and now I had a name for it. She tried to prepare me that our situation might not improve and I might need to steel myself to the fact that Mark Tomas might have to leave our home to work on his issues in a safe setting.

She did feel that my perception of the rage directed against me had another target—the absent biological mother. She urged me to face the issue straight on despite Mark Tomas' resistance. Her greatest gift to me was putting me in touch with the South Shore Adoption Support Group (later to become Adoptive Families Together {AFT}). She talked of this group of adoptive parents who had lived through similar struggles with their adoptive children. And a common thread was that many of them had adopted children of different cultures.

I remember the first meeting I attended this group. Mark Tomas was in the eighth grade and things were really escalating rapidly. I was welcomed with a big hug from Linda, the founder of the group. She immediately put me at ease by relating her experience as an adoptive parent of an Asian child. She had not had an easy time of it and was willing to speak freely about her situation. She came across as warm and affectionate, genuine and seasoned by her experiences. She possessed a strength that struck a chord with me.

Other members filtered in, all women, and the meeting began. People went around the room introducing themselves and giving background on how they had joined the group. Most of the parents in the group had seen Corrine at one time or another for help with their adoptive family. A number of the members had adopted children of a different cultural heritage than that of their own. A number had gone through painful journeys with their adopted children. A few parents were there because they had young children who had not had any difficulty, but they wanted the connection with other adoptive parents. Rather than being scared off by the veterans of teenage adoptive crises, they were there to learn what they could from the veterans' experiences, in the hopes that they might be able to prevent such a crisis in their family.

As people went around the room, they gave thumbnail sketches of their experiences. I felt a camaraderie with them. Some of them had already survived past the point of my current crisis, and they were able to talk about their story with poignancy, laughter, and some distance. This was a group of strong, caring survivors. Some had been to hell and back. And they still had the ability to laugh. They were not jaded or cynical. Some had moved beyond their own situations and were committed to opening the doors on the reality of adoptive problems and wanted to educate other parents and professionals in this field to the reality of the adoptive experience.

When my turn came, I started to tell my story and broke into tears. I told the group that I thought I was near the point of us to having our son leave our home to get the help he needed. Everyone was supportive and understood my distress. They did not minimize it; they commiserated with me. They were proof that coping with these problems was possible. They were a wealth of knowledge about placements and agency bureaucracies. But, more than that, they were the experts on issues of adoption. Through their own experiences, they had learned that many of the helpers they sought did not understand their problems. They educated themselves on the issues involved in adoption and were trying to spread that knowledge to others.

They let me know that Mark's behavior was consistent with some adolescent adoptees. They talked about the symptoms of attachment disorder, which is not uncommon with some adoptees. The symptoms they described were the very same things we had seen with Mark Tomas: substance abuse, anger, stealing, lying, poor self-esteem, and feeling very different from your family. I later thought it interesting that what they described as attachment disorder, the hospital had labeled the exact same symptoms as character disorder. They talked about the inherent systemic problems in the adoptive process. With this group, my real education about adoption began. They helped me see the connections between basic facts we know about child development and its implications for an adoptee. I had assumed that because we had adopted an infant, he would bond with us effortlessly, because we would be the first parents he would know. That presumption embarrassed me now.

Thinking about this with this new perspective made sense. Studies had shown that the unborn child recognizes its mother's voice. It is soothing and familiar. A bond has already developed prior to birth. A newborn is aware of the particular scent or smell of his/her mother. These sensations are imprinted in the baby's consciousness. I had never considered this impact or their relevance. I had set upon the task of bonding with my children. But in Mark Tomas' situation, my ignorance of that

143

previous bond was an example of the systemic problem for adoptees. An adoptive child has no control over his/her young destiny. And the adoptive parents' lack of knowledge and finesse in handling this complicated issue plays a part in setting the stage for the emergence of attachment difficulties. The high preponderance of adopted adolescents having difficulties lends credibility to the belief that identity issues are seriously influenced by the adoption triangle. Minimalizing this primal bond was not intentional, it was primarily due to ignorance.

There are ways to help a child with this. Talking openly about birth parents, sharing information about background and giving details and descriptions, asking for pictures of the biological parents, requesting a toy or article of clothing that the child can cherish and use for comfort are all things to do that can help the child. Every child needs memories and a hold on his or her past. Even unpleasant memories, carefully shared, are better than no memory. And especially important when there are transracial issues, finding cultural role models and incorporating them into your extended family network is essential.

The group also talked of the need to seek out professionals with adoption expertise. They gave me names of some of these professionals and suggested that I follow up with one of them. They suggested I put adoption issues right out on the table regardless of Mark Tomas' apparent lack of interest. They directed me back to my adoption agency to request further information. They said I would probably be pushed off, but I needed to push back to gather all the information that could be found. Corrine and her agency became the adoptive specialists for both Mark Tomas and Beth.

When I got home, I shared what I had learned at the meeting with Mark. We then asked Mark Tomas to join us. I again shared what I had learned. Then though we had told him most of what we knew about his background, we disclosed an additional piece of information. That was that he had two biological siblings. We had held this back as our adoption worker said this information would be difficult to handle. It raised the issue as to why his biological mother kept her other children but gave him up.

Next, we showed him the letters from the nun who cared for him in her convent room in Amarillo from his birth to his arrival with us. We also shared that when he was born, his mother released him for adoption, but initially, his biological father had requested that he be given custody. We discussed the reasons why the court released him for adoption after thirteen weeks. He became angry with us and said he was not interested in this information and he threw the pieces of paper we had given him to read across the table. No surprise there, what paper we had was from his initial caretaker, a nun, that was no genuine connection for him.

Within a few months, after Mark Tomas was hospitalized and then moved to various placements, Mark and I made a decision to search for his biological mother. Our search to reunion process occurred over the next two years or so. I called our adoption agency and explained that Mark had been having serious difficulty for years and now was psychiatrically hospitalized. So, we needed as much information as could be found. They agreed to call the adoption agency in Texas and to forward out request for information based on medical necessity.

After several weeks, we heard that the agency in Texas had decided to honor our request. They would attempt to locate the biological mother and let her know that we were trying to contact her. We decided to wait to see if she could be located and if she was willing to contact us before we told Mark Tomas. We did not want to raise his hopes only to have them dashed. Things moved slowly. After several phone calls to our agency and to the agency in Texas and long waits for responses to the phone calls, we finally heard what we had hoped for. The agency stated that they thought they had located the biological mother. The agency in Texas had assigned a social worker to our case and she would attempt to make contact with her in the near future. I contacted this social worker and asked if we could send an introductory letter explaining our reasons for the search as well as a letter from Mark Tomas. She said that would be all right.

When Mark Tomas came home that weekend from I.F.L.L., we shared the news with him. He was awestruck. A door, which he had been fearful of opening, was now ajar. Surprisingly, he was not angry with us. For the first time in a long time, he viewed us as his allies. I worked on composing a letter to his mom and shared it with him for his approval. He also wrote a note to send along with mine. Here is the letter I sent in care of the social worker in Texas.

Dear Mark Tomas' Mom,

I'm sure that our contacting you comes as a surprise and is totally unexpected. First of all, Mark's father and I want to thank you from the bottom of our hearts for the wonderful gift you bestowed on us by allowing us to adopt Mark Tomas. We love him so much and he has brought such joy into our lives. Despite the fact that we have never been in contact, we share a very special bond—our son, Mark Tomas. And it is for him and his well-being that we are reaching out to you. When we adopted Mark some 15 years ago, we never really thought about the fact that we would be searching for you. In fact, when Mark was young, I sometimes worried that you would change your mind and try and take him from us.

We mistakenly thought that if we just loved him and raised him, everything would be fine. We did not think about the fact that Mark had a very special bond with you that would always stay with him. Now that he is a teenager, we worry less about losing him to anyone but are more concerned with him being able to find himself, develop his own personality, and to come to peace with himself. Despite all of our love, it has been hard for Mark Tomas the last couple of years and he finds himself having a lot of emotions pulling at him that he does not fully understand.

He is proud of his Mexican-American heritage, but we have so little information to give him a sense of his background, and to build upon his pride. As white Americans in a middle-class suburban town, it is impossible to fill this need. We hope you will be able to help Mark in this endeavor to discover his beginnings, for you are his past. We are his present and together, we can help him build a future.

This may be easier if I tell you a little about Mark. He's a very handsome teenager with dark brown hair and big brown eyes that have eyelashes as long as paintbrushes! He has a wiry frame and is strong and stoic in manner. He never complains of pain. He likes to wear big, baggy clothes and loves rap music.

He is very sensitive and he has a very special way with younger children. They gravitate to him. He is not a big talker, but what he says is usually perceptive.

He has a natural ability for drawing and he has a good sense of how things work. He can look at a diagram and put something together in no time. He is more interested in the big picture more than in the little details. He is popular and makes friends easily. He is quiet but feels things deeply. He has made great strides in learning how to talk about what he feels rather than reacting first. He is a bright young man who is a plugger. Due to his learning disabilities, he must work harder than some of his classmates, and this is frustrating to him. He likes sports and has played on hockey and baseball teams since he was a little boy. He has a younger brother and sister who look up to him.

Mark has a lot of questions he would like answers to if you can share your knowledge with him. He wonders what his mom, dad, and stepsiblings look like. He is curious about what kind of personalities they are, what their interests are, their strengths, and their weaknesses. He wants to be able to compare how he sees himself with what his biological relatives are like. He also wonders whether there were any medical or emotional problems, like substance abuse or anger outbursts or learning disabilities. He would like to hear about his relatives' talents, what they like doing and what they do well. I know that this is a tall order to fill, but we can take this as slowly as everyone needs. Mark's dad and I will do all we can to help in this process. You have our warm thoughts and prayers.

We look forward to hearing from you.
Sincerely,
Mark Tomas' adoptive Mom

The process was cumbersome. We had to send the letter to the Massachusetts adoption agency, then they forwarded it to the Texas agency. The next step was for the social worker in Texas to meet with Mark's bio mom and give her the letter. The wait seemed indeterminable, especially for Mark Tomas. After a month, I called Texas to speak with the social worker at that agency. She had met with Mark's bio mom and had given her the letter. She said Mark's mom had been emotional upon reading the letter, but she reassured her that we were good people to have taken these steps in order to help our son. She reported that Mark's mother did plan on responding to us. The social worker encouraged her to seek out counseling to help her deal with this turn of events and the implications for her and her family.

Again, we waited. Mark Tomas regularly asked if a letter had come in the mail. In a few weeks, a letter did arrive for him. Mark Tomas opened the letter and began to read it—he started to cry. His immediate response was: "She does love me!". This was a very powerful moment. I joined him in the armchair and hugged him as he continued to read the letter. We were all crying now—Mark Tomas, Mark, and I.

Mark Tomas said he was so filled with emotions that he did not know what to think. His next words were poignant with meaning. He said: "I've had a big hole in my heart that has been filled." And for the first time, he said that for most of his life, he wondered about why he had been given up for adoption and if his mother had loved him. And then, he talked and talked about his feelings about being adopted that had been buried for years. This was the start of many talks about his adoption. Now he was an active participant in these discussions. And he would bring up the topic himself.

The door to his past was now wide open. He wrote back to his mother asking more questions as she had in her first letter to him, tried to answer each of the questions in his letter. I also wrote another letter and in this second letter, I filled her in with more detail regarding Mark's problems, his placements, and his progress. After we sent the second set of letters, we waited but got no response. Mark Tomas became worried and so did Mark and I. I contacted the agency in Texas, only to find out that the original social worker assigned to our case had left the agency and the case had not been reassigned.

Our letters had remained unopened on a vacant desk and had not been forward on to Mark's bio mother. I was upset at their apparent lack of sensitivity and requested that our names, addresses, and phone number be given to his mom. I also requested that we be able to contact Mark Tomas' mother directly. I felt that from this point on, we did not need intermediaries now that a link had been established. They granted my request and from that point on, we communicated directly.

When we received the first set of letters, there was an additional letter in the packet. It was from Mark Tomas' older sister welcoming him into their family. She provided lots of information about Mark Tomas' relatives and he now had an extensive family tree. Accompanying the letters were a number of pictures of his family. Mark Tomas treasured these pictures and poured over them until I feared they might fall apart.

We developed a regular communication with our Texas relatives. And Mark Tomas and his mother, sister, and younger stepbrother set about the task of getting to know one another. We progressed from letters to phone calls. After a series of phone calls, a rhythm developed of Mark Tomas talking on the phone with his Texas family every two weeks.

Mark and I had discussed and thought ahead to the next step—the reunion. We had decided that our graduation gift to Mark Tomas for all the hard work he did at his placement would be a trip to Texas, accompanied by me, to meet his family face-to-face. We had wanted to surprise him with this gift. Things progressed so fast that before our surprise, he told us his other family had invited him to Texas and he asked if was this possible. We told him of our plans for him to go to Texas with me as a graduation gift after he graduated from I.F.L.L. He was excited and eager for the time to arrive—but he still had three months before he graduated from the program.

Mark would have two reunions in a short period of time. Not sooner would he reunite with us, then we would embark on a trip to Texas to meet his other family.

Chapter 15
1996: The Journey
Home Reunification

Mark Tomas had graduated from I.F.L.L. and we were so glad to be bringing him back home. We all expected that there would be a period of adjustment before things fell into place, but we were hoping to get back to a routine of family life. Mark Tomas was a little tentative at first. He had agreed to attend summer school for one or two subjects as a way of adjusting to a more typical high school classroom in preparation for the following September. He intended to sit in for an algebra course and a Spanish 1 course. The Spanish course was cancelled because not enough people had signed up. He also intended to find some part-time work to fill his time and to make some money.

The first week home, he had too much time on his hands and talked of being 'I.F.L.L.-sick'. He was homesick for I.F.L.L. He made a number of phone calls to friends he had met in the program and who had also graduated. He made a visit to his friend, Tito, who lived in Springfield. His dad and I were aware that this was a difficult time for him. Glad as he was to be back home and out of residential placement, he had returned to a community that he had felt separate from and his time away had only reinforced that feeling. His dad and I discussed ways to help him with the transition. We decided to write a letter to friends of ours in town as well as to the parents of children he had once been friendly with several years before. Here is a copy of the letter we sent:

Dear ----------,

We wanted to let you know that we are very pleased to have Mark Tomas back home with us. It's been a long road for all of us, but it has been well worth it. After over a year, having him home brings us much joy. Mark graduated from the Institute of Family Life and Learning with high honors and even higher praise from his staff and teachers. He worked very hard while he was there and the results have paid off. We are proud of all the strides he made and all the work he did there. He has been clean and sober for over one year and has made one right choice after another. He will be attending Cathedral High School in Boston in the fall as a sophomore.

It's a difficult transition back to your community after you have been gone for a long time, but he is glad to be back home and we are all so happy to be a whole family again.

If you happen to see Mark walking down the street, he would be glad to have you stop and say 'hi'. If you are so inclined, please feel free to call to say 'hello'.

Sincerely,
Mark and Kathy Regan

Initially, there appeared to be little response to the letter. Months later, we were to learn that it did make an impression and people were genuinely pleased to hear of his progress. Some parents indicated to us that they had shared the letter with their family and encouraged their children to let him know that they were glad to see him when they ran into him. We had shown the letter to Mark and had obtained his approval prior to sending it out. We felt that everyone was aware that we had gone through 'bad times' and we wanted to bring it out in the open that he had turned things around. We were proud of him and we wanted folks to know that.

Since Mark Tomas had no one available with whom to socialize, his dad agreed to drive him to Springfield, where he could spend the weekend with his fried, Tito. He reported that Tito lived in an apartment in a low-cost housing section of Springfield. Tito greeted Mark, but he did not see a parent. He picked him up on Sunday and Mark Tomas appeared in good spirits. He reported that he had hung out with Tito and Tito's friends. Tito seemed friendly and meeting him at IFFL, he was polite and talked of wanting to get out of the program and make something of his life. He appeared to be a good influence and he and Mark Tomas clearly enjoyed being together.

It was also a time of apprehension as the following week, we were to embark on our journey to Texas. It was difficult to feel settled when such a big event was looming on the horizon. As the week wore on, the climate changed to one of eager anticipation for Mark as he was packing and preparing for the trip.

He spent time with his brother and appeared to enjoy talking, playing cards, and shooting hoops. They engaged in some horseplay, an activity that had been suspended for a long time. Though I would sometimes get nervous and fearful that the horseplay would escalate, it was pleasing to see them interacting as typical adolescent brothers. Mark Tomas also babysat for his sister one day and was the epitome of a responsible older brother. He told us often that he loved us and was glad to be home. His brother and sister were glad that he was going to Texas to meet his other family. They grew up with discussions about being a blended family and that meant that we had other family members who did not sit at our table, but they were connected to us.

I found that as our trip to Texas neared, I was apprehensive. We had made the arrangements for Mark Tomas's quest several months before; now it was close to really happening. I had a mix of emotions. I was apprehensive as to what we would find. I worried about the visit not going well and how that would affect Mark Tomas. But what I really worried most about was the visit going too well and how we would both deal with that. We had done a lot of preparation and had many contacts both by letter and by phone. His biological mother and I had several letters to each other. I had decided that even though his bio mother had extended an invitation for us to stay with them, it was important for me to have a hotel room as a home base during our stay in Texas.

At first, Mark Tomas was not enthused about the idea, but he was able to understand that this was more comfortable for me, even though he did not feel this way himself. I also made arrangements to rent a car when we arrived so I could be independently mobile. I wondered what was in store for me. I also thought that his bio mom was probably more nervous than I was. I even had some thoughts of resentment that I had to go through this. I worried that he would find his biological mother to be the fulfillment of all his fantasies and would find me lacking in comparison. Then I would tell myself to 'get a grip', that this was our reality. Mark Tomas did love me, he did love her, he needed this for his well-being and that meant our family needed this for its well-being. I knew that despite my reservations, I would do the right thing to help this reunion of families occur in the most positive way possible. I also thought of my friends in the Adoptive Families Together group and gained reassurance knowing that a number of them had already take this step and had weathered the results of the search and reunion.

From our correspondence, I had learned we had some things in common. She was family-centered, she worked, she liked to cook, and she was the main organizer of the household. She reported she was religious and was affectionate. So, we had enough in common to make some basic connection and I hoped this would help Mark Tomas in his transition between his two worlds.

Off to Texas we went. The plane ride was uneventful. We were quiet and Mark listened to music most of the trip. When we disembarked at the airport in Texas, he asked me to walk ahead of him into the airport terminal.

When he arrived at Logan Airport in Boston sixteen years ago, he was brought to me at the arrival gate. Now, here we were in Austin, Texas, and I was bringing him to his other mother at the arrival gate. I quickly searched that crowd at the gate and spotted his mother and stepbrother as they stood up and I waved. We all walked towards each other, joined, and then hugged. We were happy, apprehensive, and all more than a little nervous. I think this saved us from a big, emotional scene. We agreed that it had been easy to recognize each other from the pictures we had sent back and forth. Mark's mother and stepbrother came with us as we picked up the rental car and then they followed us to the hotel. We talked for a while in the hotel room and then, we left and followed them to their home.

They lived about twenty minutes outside the city in a small suburban town that was primarily Mexican-American in composition. Their home was small, very clean and had a wonderful aroma of Mexican spices that greeted you as you entered. Mark's mother's husband, who was home from work and had been awaiting our arrival, greeted us. The family was very hospitable and warm. His mom had cooked a typical Mexican-American meal of meat, beans, rice, and tacos. We ate and talked around the kitchen table. After dinner, Mark's stepsister and her daughter came over, accompanied by her fiancé. We all talked together, then the younger generation went out to show Mark Tomas the town and to talk by themselves. Mark's mom's husband said good night and went to bed. Mark's mom and I talked for several hours. She talked a lot about Mark Tomas and she had a lot of questions about his life.

The kids finally returned and Mark Tomas and I left to go back to the hotel. It was 1:30 in the am when we got back to our room! Even though it was late, we were both too wound up to immediately fall asleep. We compared notes on our perceptions of how the initial visit had gone and we both agreed it was a wonderful start. Mark Tomas said that although initially he had been nervous, he was surprised at how quickly he had become comfortable. He felt he got along well with his younger stepbrother and liked his best friend, who he had met when they all went on a car ride. I should mention that accurately sorting out siblings and stepsiblings was a difficult for me. I learned that Mark had an older brother, who was not present during this visit. This older brother had the same biological father as Mark Tomas. His older sister did not have the same father. Mark's younger brother was the product of his mother's current husband.

It also appeared that even though his mom and her dad appeared happy that there had been separations within their relationship. It was confusing for me and I was never sure if Mark Tomas was able to sort out the intricacies of how he was related to whom, when, and who was growing up in the home with his mother at different points in time. His sister was the person who appeared to have the history of the family and was clearer in answering questions. I didn't want to seem as if I was prying, and Mark's mother wanted to present things in a positive perspective.

The next morning, we got up, showered, dressed, and returned to his mother's home. Mark had packed some clothes in case he decided to spend the night there. When we arrived, his mother had prepared a big breakfast of heuvos rancheros, sausage, beans, and tortillas. Mark surprised himself by eating the sausage and the beans and liked them both. This was adventurous for him as he was somewhat of a picky eater and often would not try new things based upon appearance and smell.

We talked together for a while and then went out to see a movie. The boys saw one picture and his mother and I saw another. His mother shared with me her life circumstances when Mark was born and the reasons leading up to her placing him for adoption. She discussed her feelings after he was adopted and the regret she had lived with after making that decision. She talked of how important this reunion was to her as was her families' acceptance of Mark's arrival. That last part was clear; he was welcomed into their family as if he had been there all his life. I felt that they also treated me with affection and respect.

This second day was difficult for me. The newness of the situation had worn off. I was happy and sad at the same time. Seeing Mark Tomas sitting on the couch with his stepbrother, they looked so much alike. He looked as if he belonged here. He looked happy and relaxed. Nor could I miss his resemblance to his mother. He had her eyes and her body type. For all their attempts of including me, he fit in and I felt like an outsider. A small part of me was sad that he looked so happy with them. I questioned whether he had even been really happy with us in all the years that we had raised him. I was asked a lot of questions about our family and Mark's brother and sister. A suggestion was made that the next visit should include our entire families.

In discussing Mark's difficulties, his mother stated she thought adoption issues played a large part. She felt the anger Mark had displayed towards me was really his anger at her for allowing him to be adopted. She thanked me for our efforts to get help for Mark and she said that he had reported to her that his days of getting in trouble were over. She also related the previous night after we had left, she and her children talked of their past experiences and shared the bad times they had been through and their hopes for the future.

The first two days of the reunion were over. They had been intense but fruitful. I learned from Mark Tomas that the kids felt that the mothers needed to get to know one another, so they had purposely left us alone for hours at a time so it would be easier for us to build a relationship. We were both trying so hard that it was draining for both of us. Mark did decide to spend the night with his other family and I drove back to the hotel.

I did find that when I returned to the hotel, I had a strong need for quiet time. First, I called Mark and then Debbie with an update and then turned on the television. But even movies on the television had no appeal. I reflected on the day and then did some reading until I was able to fall asleep.

After the first night, Mark Tomas continued to stay with his Texas family. I would join them for dinner and then drive back to the hotel. Mark and I had little time alone to talk, but I knew he was trying to fill every minute of this new experience and I did not begrudge him this opportunity. He and his step-siblings always checked with both mothers before making plans and several times, he let me know he loved me and was glad I was part of this process.

Mark reported to me that his younger stepbrother and his sister's fiancée had told him that by the time he left, he would feel he was part of the Chicano race and he would feel his heritage inside of him. He joined their daily activities and was able to experience what their day-to-day existence was like. He was able to feel what it felt like to be Chicano in a way that was impossible to experience within our family. He was able to feel comfortable in his skin for the first time. He was also able to see that life here was not always easy. His mother stressed to him and his younger stepbrother that unless they obtained an education, they would not be able to get good jobs and have a better life.

His sister took me aside one day to tell me that she shared with Mark Tomas that their life was very hard at times and that she envied the opportunities he had been granted and that she felt he should be grateful to me and his father. She also hinted to me that her mother was painting a rosier picture to Mark Tomas than was actually the case. She conveyed to me a sense that she was concerned to some degree about some of the things their mother was saying to Mark Tomas. (I was to find out later that his bio mom told him if she knew he would be adopted by a white Catholic family that lived up North, she never would have released him for adoption. She had questioned me about Mark's difficulties and our attempts to get him help and I answered truthfully. I also learned at a later point in time that she told Mark Tomas that she loved him as he was and she never would have put him on medication.)

The third and fourth days, I called Mark Tomas and encouraged him to spend time with his mother. I wanted him to have time with his other family and to know that I trusted him and that I was OK with them strengthening their bond without my being there. I came to their home in the evenings for dinner. One night, we played Gestures and had a good time. Another night, we watched movies together. One Saturday, Mark's stepfather was able to get time off and we all went to San Antonio. It was hot—100 degrees! We spent the day at Fiesta Texas, a Six Flags theme park. Then we spent the evening in downtown San Antonio and ate at a great Mexican restaurant, Mi Entierre, where we feasted on great food and listened to a Mariachi band.

Mark Tomas became quite blue during this meal; he was quiet and looked sad. It had hit him that the visit was nearly over and he was felling a sense of loss. When we got back to their home later, he was able to discuss his feelings. His family members all reassured him that when this visit came to a close, it was only the end of the beginning. He readjusted his mindset and enjoyed the remaining two days before our departure. After I left to return to the hotel, the family stayed up late talking. Sunday afternoon, the family celebrated Mark Tomas's birthday with a cookout. There was a piñata filled with candies, and a barbeque. Friends and relatives were invited.

As I left that night, I wondered how Mark Tomas would handle his last day with this other family. I was fearful he might tell me he did not want to return home with me and I did not know what I would do if this happened. I called him Monday morning from the hotel and encouraged him to spend some time alone with his mother that day as we were leaving the following morning. I suggested that he start to pack his things and asked him if he thought he would be able to do that. He related that he had also thought about this and how difficult it would be, but that he thought he would be able to do it.

He said that he had decided to come back with me to the hotel this evening rather than sleep in his family's home. I went over that evening for dinner and we departed for the hotel at 11 pm. After dinner, a phone call was made to his grandparents, who lived in West Texas and they told Mark Tomas that they hoped to meet him on his next visit. Our departure was on everyone's mind and we were all trying to make the parting as easy as was possible. Our goodbyes were brief and we made plans for his mother and stepbrother to meet us at the hotel in the morning.

We had breakfast together at the hotel and they followed us to the airport. We said our goodbyes at the gate and talked of visits to come. On the flight back, Mark Tomas surprised me with his ability to talk about his stay. I thought he would be sad and quiet, and I feared he might be resentful that we were returning home. He was hopeful and looking forward to future visits. In fact, he talked of his hopes to return at Christmas and then again, the following summer. He voiced his desire to live in Texas when he finished high school. I told him that his dad and I would probably not have problems at his moving to Texas after high school if he was going to college there. If he went to school in Austin, he would be very close to his family and could see them often. I reminded him that his mother had stressed the importance of his going to college to both he and his younger stepbrother.

Then I was pleased to hear Mark state that as hard as it was to leave, he was looking forward to seeing his father, his brother, and sister. He admitted that he had missed them. I drew a big sigh of relief. Things were working out. He seemed peaceful rather than sad and he was on the road to putting the pieces of his life together. He did see himself as part of two families that were now connected.

Chapter 16
Moving On

There was no perceptible letdown after our return from Texas. I was aware that we had but a month and a half left of summer before the pace would pick up. It was a brief hiatus before each child would pick up their compasses and continue on their own paths of discovery.

Mark Tomas had now been reunited with his Texas family and I hoped a bond between us would grow and be a positive one. Only time would tell if he had been able to integrate these two parts of himself into a comfortable identity.

Our family was still growing and changing. Mark Tomas was still in the throes of his adolescence and Andy was right on his heels. Beth had her search for a meaningful identity ahead of her. Each of them was a very different personality and each had different issues.

Mark Tomas had been able to clearly identify his main focus. His cultural heritage was in the forefront as the issue around which his identity lied. Andy was the middle child, biological, and sandwiched between his adoptive brother and sister. He had no clearly burgeoning issues to center his development around. His growth was more subtle as he absorbed the environment around him, taking in what was appealing and ignoring what was not. He was people-centered and valued highly how people reacted to him. Beth was the youngest child, was the girl, and was adopted. She had tremendous perseverance. She had observed Mark and his struggles with his identity and I hoped that might prove helpful to her in the upcoming years.

Her bond with me had a very different flavor than was Mark Tomas's with me at her age. This I hoped would prove helpful when she confronted her adoptive past head-on. My wish was that we could work together and she would not feel that she must struggle with me to claim her past. She had seen us incorporate Mark Tomas's other family into our life and knew we are ready to explore this with her when she is interested in doing this.

Mark and I shifted between being a stabilizing presence and being flexible enough to adapt to changes we must all make to help our children grow and find a place for themselves that meets their needs and is comfortable for them. I felt that we must continue to strive for resilience, wisdom, and most of all, humor. I was firmly convinced that that there was a positive correlation between levity and sanity.

Mark Tomas and Andy would be attending new schools. They both picked schools outside the town in which we lived. They chose remarkably different types of schools and that would influence their interests, their friendships, as well as where they would be spending much of their time.

Mark Tomas chose a Catholic High School in the inner city, which was noted for its cultural diversity. He would not be a minority at this school, as the student population was comprised of students who were Hispanic, Black, and Asian, and had representatives from thirty different countries. The school prided itself on providing an atmosphere in which students from these varied backgrounds 'can learn and develop respect and have appreciation for one another across lines of race, color, sex, and creed'.

Andy chose a Catholic High School in the city, which was more traditional, had a generally middle-class student body, was Jesuit-run and stressed academic and moral development.

They both would have a long day involving commuting after school activities and an increased homework load. Beth would have to adjust to her brothers spending less time at home and being less available to her on a daily basis. Our lives would be busy with everyone going in separate directions, yet we would need to build in a way to have time together so we can share in the joys and tribulations of each person's endeavors.

We had traveled a long way over the past four plus years. A lot had changed in our lives and a lot had remained the same. I did not know at this point in time, what lied ahead for us. Our journey thus far brought out the worst in us and the best in us.

Hopefully, we had grown from our experiences. I expected there would most likely be some setbacks for us moving forward from here. But I hoped we all had the desire to avoid the pitfalls if we were able to see them coming. Where we had been may only be a way station and not our final destination. It seemed to me that we needed to live in the present with our past experiences to guide us.

Chapter 17
1996 – 2000: Spiraling Downhill

Things did move on, but not in a way I had hoped or expected. Mark Tomas started his Sophomore year at Cathedral High. Initially, I had high hopes. He appeared to be going to school daily and he joined the football team. We were pleased to attend his games in the fall. His first semester marks were mainly Cs, with a couple of Ds. He was put in a special study group that was mentored by successful businessmen who were graduates of Cathedral High.

As we had planned the upcoming Christmas after Mark's reunion in Texas, we made arrangements for Mark Tomas to fly to Texas to visit with his family over the holidays. The trip began inauspiciously with his plane being rerouted to the Midwest due to bad weather. He spent the night with other passengers on his plane in an airport waiting for the plane to continue on in the am. He called us from the airport and we were apprehensive that he was alone and hoped that things would get back on track in the morning. He had called his mother in Texas to inform her of the delay and she reported that his stepsister would meet him at the gate in Austin the following day.

He did arrive late Christmas eve. I was worried throughout this visit as Mark Tomas was not calling us and I had to call his mother repeatedly. Each time I called, I was told that Mark was out, but that everything was fine. I was uncomfortable about what was actually happening during this visit and I was not able to get a clear picture from his mother about their daily activities.

I was relieved that he did speak with me on the phone the night before his departure there. This time on his return from Texas, he was close-mouthed and had little to say. He also appeared sad though he denied this. I found out much later that during this visit, Mark had asked his mother if he could stay and live with them. She told him that this was not possible, that he needed to wait until he finished high school and could get a full-time job to be able to support himself.

I am sure he perceived this as a second rejection by her. He talked less about his Texas family and I could see that phone calls and letters had stopped. His adoption therapist said that many second reunions led to disappointment and sadness over the reality of what could never be. They most often did not live up to the child's fantasies and expectations. I began to suspect that my hopes of Mark Tomas integrating his two families into a cohesive whole were just that—my hopes and less likely to be a realistic outcome.

By the end of Mark Tomas' sophomore year at Cathedral, the school let us know that Mark was not invited back because they were unprepared to manage him. They felt he needed more specialized services. They reported that he was often absent or would leave the campus early in the day. They also said that he was not completing his homework. He did not pass any of his subjects that second semester. We were not surprised as he was not coming home after school and was staying out late and would not answer any questions regarding what he was doing and where he was going. He reported that "he was with friends in Roxbury". He would offer no specifics and would become angry with our questions about how he was spending his time. Andy and Beth knew nothing of 'these friends'; they were never included in his excursions, and all three children had different social circles.

That summer, we struggled to find a school that would accept him and a charter school in a nearby community agreed to let him enter as a sophomore in September. Mark begrudgingly agreed to attend. I would drop him off in the morning and then go on to my work. He was uncommunicative as to how things were going. And once again, he was not coming home after school but staying out later and later in the evenings with no response when asked where he was spending his time.

We were back in familiar and unpleasant territory as Mark Tomas began to escalate and was now a larger teenager. His

163

therapist, Tim, called to give me another Tarasoff warning, which meant Mark was making homicidal statements about me. And again, we were advised to hide our checkbooks and credit cards and hide any knives we had. Mark did not appear to have much of a reaction to this and a closely followed third Tarasoff warning. I took them more seriously and these were specific to me. Mark's adoption therapist thought we needed to arrange for his second psychiatric hospitalization and also suggested that future plans would require a therapeutic residential school that specialized in adoption and acting out behavior.

During this second but brief hospitalization, she helped us develop a contract that spelled out our expectations for Mark and listed what he could expect from us, his parents. Mark was hospitalized on an adolescent psychiatric unit for five days in a psychiatric hospital located in a suburb of Boston. Not much was accomplished except that Mark did agree to sign the contract as a contingency for his returning home. When his father and I picked him up on the day he was being discharged, he was very angry and during the car ride home, he would not speak to us. I remember being actually frightened by the looks he was giving us.

We arrived home and had lunch after which Mark Tomas stated that he needed some fresh air and was going out for a short while. He had not returned by dinner. At approximately 6:30 that evening, Andy reported that a police car was pulling up the driveway. We asked Andy and Beth to go upstairs to their bedrooms and told them we would let them know what was happening after we had talked to the police. The police rang the front door and they requested to speak with us. The officers requested that we sit down before they explained why they were here. After sitting down in the living room, the officers identified themselves and then one officer reported: "Your son, Mark has been arrested for assaulting two boys in downtown Hingham. The boys are aged 10 and 11. They reported that they had been walking down the street in the downtown section of our town on their way home from school.

"The boys stated that they saw an older teenager at the far end of the street they were on and that he was jumping up and down and yelling at no one in particular. They were going to go down a different street, because they thought this person was acting weird. But he stopped and just started walking towards them. As he approached them, he pulled a knife out of his pocket and began threatening them. One boy started to move away, but they are alleging that Mark approached the boy who was closer and jabbed him with a knife. The boys ran away, went home, and told their parents. The parents called the police. The police, after obtaining a description of the perpetrator, began searching for him. He was located not far from where the incident occurred and was apprehended. He has been placed in lock-up at the Hingham police station and will be arraigned at the Hingham District Court in the morning."

Mark and I informed the police that Mark Tomas had just been released from an adolescent psychiatric hospital that morning. They said we would be allowed to drop off clothes and prescribed medication, which Mark did later that evening. Then Mark contacted a lawyer, someone I knew from my Adoption Support Group and she agreed to represent Mark Tomas and said she would meet us in court in the morning.

We arrived at court the following morning and Mark was arraigned. The case was continued; a trial date was set, and he was released on bail. He was put on a restraining order to avoid any contact with the victims and to avoid the downtown area.

We heard from the charter school Mark Tomas was attending. They informed us that Mark Tomas was not handing in assignments, often was not in class. And they were preparing to suspend him, as they suspected he was spending most of his day at the far end of the school grounds selling marijuana. They had been contacted by the police and had told them of their suspicions. Mark Tomas's attorney with our permission obtained the psychiatric record from the adolescent unit. She informed us that she was livid upon reading the record. It was documented that he had expressed homicidal ideation towards us, his parents, up to and including the day of discharge. She said: "You need to prepare yourselves that it is likely the judge will remand Mark Tomas to the custody of DYS," (the Division of Youth Services).

The judge did sentence Mark Tomas to the DYS with an initial stay at the Boston Facility for a 90-day evaluation to determine his level of danger to others. That report would determine which facility he would be placed in. Mark made no eye contact with us in court, and I was upset and crying. His attorney instructed me that I was not to cry and if I needed to go to the rest room to gain composure, I should do so. (I'm not sure I ever understood why it was so important for a mother not to show her distress at the reality of what was occurring and its impact of its outcome for our family.)

I did receive the support of one mother who was in court with her daughter. She approached me and said: "I'm here with Teresa, who is also having some difficulty, but my heart goes out to you. I know you have been having a very difficult time and I will keep you in my prayers". I genuinely appreciated her having the courage to come up to me with her kind words. Her daughter was in the Junior High with Mark Tomas, so she like most people in our small town knew all about Mark's troubles. It was such a routine for Mark Tomas to be in trouble that it was part and parcel of Andy and Beth's life. They each had a group of friends who accepted them as friends and their older brother's behavior did not effect that acceptance as they were now in junior high school or high school.

As Mark Tomas was sent to a DYS facility on the grounds of the old Boston State Hospital, we were now entering into the realm of corrections, a penal facility for minors. Mark was not cooperating, so the three-month evaluation lasted almost four and a half to five months. His probation officer, adoption therapist, and psychologist all contributed their perspectives. His sentence was for three years based on mandatory sentencing guidelines. Part of me was very disappointed, but another part of me was vastly relieved. We had shown that we had no ability to effectively set limits on Mark's behavior and here I believed that Mark would be safe, watched, treated, and schooled. After the evaluation was completed, the determination was for Mark Tomas to be placed in a juvenile wing of Plymouth House of Correction, an adult male prison. He was there almost a year. It was then decided that he be moved to a DYS group home facility only a few towns away from us, for the remainder of his sentence.

Andy and Beth tried very hard to have a normal life, going to school, seeing friends, participating in sports, etc. But truth be told, they were affected by all this turmoil. Andy hung out with his childhood friends, but I worried that although adolescent boys aren't usually communicative, this group of childhood friends seemed like an amorphous blob. I couldn't tell where one began and the other ended. The four boys genuinely enjoyed being together, but they seemed to me to mainly communicate in grunts and three-word phrases. Andy received a good education at Boston College High School, but he never really connected with the kids there except for one boy with whom he became friends.

Beth had shown signs of nervousness when Mark was escalating at home when she was in elementary school. Elementary school was difficult for her socially. She was a tomboy who loved sports and was not into any girly things. In fact, it was a chore to get her to wear a dress twice a year for Christmas and Easter. The girls didn't include her in the girl groups; she was never invited over to sleepovers. It made me sad.

I remember one birthday party when she was about eight or nine, it was a warm day at the end of May and I had arranged outdoor games for the girls before the cake and ice cream. We were outside and a car came up the driveway. I went to see who it was. The woman got out of the car and told me she was the mother of one of the girls, I forget which girl it was.

The mother looked at me and said: "I've come to get my daughter. I did not realize when I accepted the invitation that Beth was the sister of Mark Regan. I don't want my daughter here and I am picking her up now." I do have to report that when Beth arrived at the Junior High, things were totally different. Beth had spent her early years playing sports with the boys at our house whether they wanted her to or not. And she was good in sports, better than a number of the boys. When she got to Junior High, all the girls wanted to be her friend as she knew all the older boys who had played with her brothers. And the coaches wanted her on their teams as she excelled in sports.

My sleep vastly improved when Mark was admitted to this DYS residential community program just one town away from us. I knew well this pattern. When he was home, we were happy to be reunited as a family, but this joy was short-lived. Within a short while, things would start spiraling downhill and then I would wait for the axe to fall. The reality was that his problems, with whatever perspective you used to look at them, were too severe to be managed in a home setting. And although the needed separation would make his attachment problems even worse, that was the reality.

He was safe, the community was safe, and they had much better control over the situation then we had up until this point. We could pay more attention to our other two children, who I felt did not deserve having to be put on a back burner every time we were having massive problems with their brother.

Mark was at this facility for the remainder of his high school years. Initially, we were told there would be no contact for six weeks, giving Mark Tomas time to settle in and learn about the program. By now, that sounded familiar. Then, we would be allowed visits for a few hours. There would be family meetings, but this time, the meetings were only for Mark Tomas, Mark, and me. I was glad that Andy and Beth were not being dragged to more meetings where the total focus was their brother. This had been our previous experience when he was at the Institute for Family Living and Learning (IFLL).

The therapist assigned to us was easy to talk with about our experiences. She also was able to engage Mark Tomas in discussions. Over the course of time, we reached a point where Mark Tomas was going to make amends for his actions. His father and I were asked what events struck in our minds. His father talked of Mark's anger and not being able to reach him and his feelings about Mark Tomas's wasted potential. I recounted my love for him but my increasing fear about his anger toward me. I asked Mark Tomas if he remembered coming after me with a frying pan of hot bacon grease, or coming after me with a bat. But especially frightening was finding my bedroom, with slices in my pillow and gouges in my bureau, with a large knife on my side of the bed. Mark said he didn't recall any of those events, but he vividly remembered coming into our bedroom in the middle of the night with a big knife and standing over me with the knife and wondering what it would feel like to plunge the knife into me while I was sleeping.

You can guess my reaction. I was very upset that my son spent time entertaining serious thoughts about killing me. And he shared this memory in such a blasé manner. How horrible a parent must I have been to have a son who was so angry at me that he thought about killing me? Another part of me thought how unfair this was. I had bestowed ample quantities of love, explored every avenue available to get help and the result was that he was so angry that he often entertained serious thoughts of killing me.

I never had anticipated when I so desired to create a family that this would be my experience. And how do you deal with a child who you love, who you fear, and who you feel has turned your life upside down? At one point, the therapist pointed out that in each session, Mark Tomas and Mark sat relatively close to one another and I was on the other side, often somewhat hunched over appearing to hold my stomach. She said she had consulted with her supervisor and an outside consultant; their view was that my experiences had resulted in my having a significant Post Traumatic Stress Disorder.

And Mark and Mark Tomas seemed more aligned with one another leaving me outside their circle and that they did not seem really connected to what my experience had been like. And what was I to do with this analysis. If a man is abusive to his wife or girlfriend, the advice is to get out of the relationship and stay safe. But there are no clear directives regarding how to stay safe when the abuser was your child! I know that when Mark or Mark Tomas expressed anger or their voices raised, I would get an anxious knot in my stomach or I would sometimes just zone out. My mind went somewhere else.

It was during therapy sessions here that we learned Mark Tomas had started abusing alcohol and drugs at the age of eleven and that he stored his empty bottles within our walls. This led to our returning from one session and searching the house. We found that in all closets and crawl spaces Mark Tomas had gained access to the fiberglass insulation behind the walls and had deposited many empty bottles of beer and hard liquor buried in the fiberglass insulation. I was amazed at the collection he had hidden. And I wondered where all this drinking was taking place. I only remembered a handful of times when he was staggering drunk. As for the drug use, I was aware when he came home stoned; his eyes were red, but he never appeared to be stoned on other drugs. Maybe I was not able to identify the signs of his being under the influence of other substances. We also learned during this time that while

Mark had been in a previous program (IFLL), appearing to be successful in meeting all the goals of the program, he had, in reality, joined the ranks of the 'Latin Kings'. I wondered if this transpired when he was in House 3 and was given more freedom. I also wondered if Tito was his initial connection to the 'Latin Kings'.

The 'Latin Kings' were a gang of Hispanic members that were active in Connecticut, Massachusetts, and parts of New York, New Jersey, and California. In Massachusetts, this gang was prevalent in Lawrence, Springfield, and Brockton, cities with large Hispanic populations. The 'Latin Kings' were considered to be violent, dangerous and focused on drug dealing, extortion, and other criminal behaviors. It was deflating and demoralizing to realize that while we and program officials at IFLL were praising Mark Tomas for the strides he was making in the program, there was another sub-strata and culture co-existing within the program where some residents were outwardly appearing compliant while continuing to pursue criminal behavior. He was also able to get a number of tattoos that reflected his membership in the gang. He had a lion on his chest and he had some symbol in the webbing between two of his fingers indicating that he dealt drugs.

Though I had seen these tattoos, I was never sure when he procured them. (I did not learn till a number of years later that they were signs alerting others that he was a 'Latin King' member. I learned this at an in-service where a police officer talked about gangs and tattoos.)

Mark appeared to be following the rules of his current DYS program. By now, he had become a master at surviving in programs that were highly structured. Nearing the end of his stay, our town's high school graduation was being held for Mark's original class. The program applied for Mark Tomas to be granted a high school diploma from the local high school and sent in their educational reports. The school agreed to grant a diploma from the high school. Mark was granted a day pass to participate in the high school graduation and attend a celebratory dinner following the event. I was glad to see Mark participate in this milestone, but I also felt melancholy in that his high school years were so markedly different from all his peers. It was also awkward to be there as his actions were the talk of the town. Some people avoided us, but I was very thankful to the parents who had the courage to approach us and congratulate Mark and conveyed their unspoken sympathy to me.

I was moved and surprised by the people who did approach us—not parents of children that Mark had been friends with in earlier years—but people with whom we were not close, but who had big hearts and extended their hands to us. I was especially grateful to the Director of Special Educational Services in our town as she had been paramount in our securing a cost share with the Department of Education to fund the educational components of the programs Mark attended. And Mrs. Fish was ultimately responsible for agreeing to grant Mark a High School diploma from a respected suburban public high school. Upon Mark's graduation, I sent a dozen red roses to her at her office. Mark Tomas was due to come home about six months later. Mark was released from the DYS group home later that summer. To the best of my knowledge, during these years, Mark Tomas did not have any contact with his Texas family.

Chapter 18
2000 – 2008: Mark Tomas' Adult Years and My Moving On

Mark Tomas's coming home after years of living away from us was a big adjustment for everyone. He knew he needed to establish a structured lifestyle and finding a job was a first step. He was also expected to attend AA meetings and meet with a psychiatrist. His father called people he knew in the town who owned small businesses to see if they would give Mark a chance for employment as a friendly overture. One very kind man, Dennis, agreed to employ Mark in his warehouse. Mark worked diligently and productively for almost six months and then things began to slip. He began skipping work and eventually, he was fired after being given several attempts to improve.

He was again disappearing for periods of time and though he had no viable source of income, he was buying clothes. As you can guess, it was only a matter of time before the police were at our door with more bad news. This time, it was worse. Mark was now over eighteen; he was no longer a juvenile, and his actions were even more serious. We were informed that he had been arrested in a nearby city with two other young adults for stabbing a homeless man. This crime made little sense. The men he was with came from a different part of the state and Mark did not know them. Somehow, they got into an argument with this older homeless individual and it resulted in Mark stabbing this man. There is little I can say about how upset I was again with his behavior. I knew in my heart that it was not possible for Mark Tomas to live with us and for us to be able to have any semblance of a normal life. We just went from one bad event to another.

Mark Tomas was sentenced to prison and I think the sentence was for 18 months. Things get blurred for the next decade. Mark was in prison more that he was free throughout his twenties. He was arrested and convicted of drug dealing (heroin), carrying a gun, shoplifting, and assault. He spent time in Plymouth, Dedham, Walpole, Shirley, Souza-Baranowski (maximum security), and Suffolk County House of Correction. The bottom line was that if I included the DYS facilities, I had visited Mark in over eight penal institutions. I knew the routine: drive to the prison, leave valuables in the car, no jackets or sweaters, no sleeveless dresses, no plunging necklines and no phones, no pocketbooks, and carry your license in your hand or pocket. Then there was waiting in lines to go through metal detectors, then to be escorted through loud metal double doors, and take the elevator to the visiting area and wait your turn.

Yet for all this effort, the visits were totally strained. Where Mark Tomas was able to carry on a conversation with his father, he became totally stilted and retreated to platitudes and 'gansta' rap with me. It was always a version of: "Yo, I'm gonna show you, just you wait. I'll make you proud of me. It'll be aight." When I would ask what he was doing, how he was spending his time, the response would be, "Nuttin'". Sometimes, he would not be able to even make this effort and would just glare at me. At some point, I admitted to myself that these visits were not doing anything positive for either of us. I realized finally that my very presence made him worse. He was relaxed with his father.

And as parents, we had such different views as to what was in Mark's best interest. I had always said to the children that "you have the right to think whatever you want, but you do not have the right in words and or actions to hurt other people". I believed he had serious mental health issues and substance abuse issues. Both of these factors contributed to his inhibition and his propensity for violence. Therefore, in my estimation, these problems needed treatment and follow-up, both to aid him and to protect others. His father would listen to my reasoning, but when push came to shove, he was not able to consistently put stipulations and conditions on bailing Mark Tomas out or enforcing guidelines when he lived in our home. I think Mark felt that Mark Tomas was not capable of following through so he didn't push it. But he felt he had to be there for Mark Tomas regardless.

During these years, he sometimes lived with his girlfriend in the Lawrence area, or with 'friends', and sometimes, in shelters. I think he met his girlfriend on one of his travels to Lawrence. He and his girlfriend had children. I had hoped that being a father might somehow rein him in, but that was not the case. While we were still in living in Hingham, he would drop in and stay for a day or two, but he was out on his own. I also remember during this time, we would occasionally answer the phone and some male would be making threats that he would do harm if he did not get his money. On a few occasions, when Mark was in different prisons, he would send a letter home and within it was another letter addressed to persons in New Jersey. He would request we forward the letters. I threw them in the trash and I suspected it was 'Latin King' communications and that he was acting as an intermediary.

On one occasion, when he dropped in, he appeared very agitated and manicky. He was talking a blue streak, but most of what he was saying made little sense. Then he began bragging of having guns and of having killed people. I knew he obtained guns, but I doubted his story of having killed people. I knew he was involved in drugs and dealing, but I did not think he was a high-level gang member. What I did think of that visit was that he was probably high on some drug and that it had pushed him over into a temporary psychotic state. His behavior and his words were bizarre. He was on a rant and did not want to be interrupted. After about 90 minutes of this, he decided to leave.

His father genuinely believed that it was his mission in life to save Mark—at all costs. And those costs became exorbitant. I was of the belief that if Mark was continually bailing out Mark Tomas with no expectations of regulations to which Mark Tomas needed to agree, Mark Tomas would never learn how to control his behavior. Things had been going from bad to worse for over a decade. He had not yet learned that rules also applied to him. Knowing the rules was not enough; you had to obey the rules. You had to think of the effect of your actions on other people.

Chapter 19
2000 – 2013: Changing My Course

Our marriage suffered greatly under the stress of a child with special needs compounded by violence and substance abuse. The crux of the stress though was that we were not a united front, we were not on the same page, and over the years, our differences in what was needed grew. As our differences grew, so did our moving in separate directions. We shared less and less; we hadn't shared happy times together in years. Mark seemed only able to share one emotion with me and that was anger. I had grown tired of anger, no, that is not true; I actually began to get a sick feeling when he expressed his anger. I felt that I had experienced enough anger from my son and husband to last me several lifetimes. Mark's anger was verbal rants over what one of the children had done; ninety-five percent of the time, it was Mark. But he worked through his anger by venting in front of me. The children saw little of it.

When I realized that we were growing emotionally more apart year by year, I began to think about divorce. We had made a commitment to raise a family and I felt that commitment overrode my self-interest. It seemed especially important as we had children by birth and by adoption. I believed that they were entitled to an intact family. I began thinking about making a life for myself, but I knew that I needed to wait until they were approaching adulthood. We communicated compatibly around the children, planned holiday events and meals, and participated in sharing holidays with our relatives. I honestly think that our children, now grown, have happy memories of those times.

When Beth, our youngest, left for college, it was time for me to begin to plan what my future life would be like. Andrew was already out of the home and was independent.

I did talk with Mark on a number of occasions stating that we were both unhappy and we both deserved better than what we had been dealt. I stated that our marriage was just not strong enough to withstand all the stress our lives entailed. We did try couple's therapy, but that was not helpful at all. The therapist thought we just needed to figure out how to compromise. That made no sense to me and how do you compromise when your basic values and beliefs are markedly different? We had disagreed for years on an approach in dealing with our son and despite my being a psychiatric nurse, my views and beliefs were rarely taken and followed.

I believed that one of the long-standing problems was that Mark Tomas always blamed me for his first psychiatric hospitalization and saw that as the beginning of his demise. He hated being viewed as having psychiatric problems. I think his father felt guilty about this. He was never able to take a lasting stand on the need for Mark Tomas to follow through with psychiatric appointments and AA and NA meetings. And there was the larger issue of me being the scapegoat for the rage he had directed at his biological mother. I also think that Mark was depressed and had been for a number of years. I attempted to talk about this and my thoughts were tolerated but not highly valued. His was very disappointed in where his life had gone and it was so far from his hopes and dreams.

I began a process that was aimed towards the future. I established my own checking account, and Mark and I were now paying bills separately. I felt this was important because when we had a joint account and I said I would not agree to more legal fees to spend to defend Mark Tomas in further legal charges, Mark went ahead and spent the money anyhow. I found that when we were having major disagreements about important issues, Mark had been lying to me and doing what he thought was best behind my back. It was upsetting to balance trying to do this eventual divorce without acrimony when I had been lied to and ignored. I began to mention to Andy and Beth that their father and I had grown apart and that we were thinking about a separation.

I actually gave them this information about two years before we did separate. For the first year after giving them this news, both children were angry with me. I had the support of some good friends where I worked, especially my friend Kathy. They were helpful and gave me the perspective that in time, my children would come around. And they were correct. With some time, both were able to see that they had their memories and continued to have loving relationships with both of their parents, so although disappointed, all of our lives were continuing on.

I contacted an attorney and her advice was that getting a formal separation prior to obtaining a divorce was adding an extra step if there was no hope of reconciliation. After thirty years of marriage, Mark was served with divorce papers. He never made any attempt to see if I would change my mind; there were no pronouncements of love or request for another chance. He was able to agree that it was very sad and that we both deserved better than the cards we had been dealt.

It was a year before we had our actual day in court and the divorce was granted. It was to be finalized in ninety days following our court appearance. In that year, we had a number of tasks to accomplish to get the house ready for sale. I had been spending weekend days over the previous year looking at condos and smaller homes in a nearby town on the Atlantic Ocean. I liked the town and I felt it was a good fit for me starting a new phase of my life. I loved spending time at the beach and Nantasket Beach was a place I spent much time every summer. It was one of the places where I found peace and beauty.

When we sold our home and I moved to the next town, Mark returned to Boston, the city where his family resided. I loved his family and had felt a part of them for the past thirty years, but they were gone to me now. And truth be told, Mark loved and needed his brothers and sisters. And their duty was with him, not me. I saw myself as being more resilient than Mark and more able to make it on my own. And as our emotional distance grew, I felt like I had been on my own for years though we resided in the same house. I had a sense of freedom now. I didn't have to worry about what someone else would think if I bought a new dress, went out to eat, or decided to take a vacation. I was accountable only to myself. I was tired of regretting what I did not have. It was time to take care of myself. I was fortunate to have some wonderful girlfriends whose support I felt in or out of their presence. I had activities I participated in a gym in a nearby town and met women in water aerobics and Zumba with whom I socialized monthly. My life fell into a new pattern that became familiar.

Would Mark and I had been able to make a go of our marriage if we did not have the stress of the challenges in raising a very troubled and angry child? I can't say for sure, but I think we still would not have made it. Mark appeared to me to deal with disappointment by shutting down most of his positive emotions towards me. I don't really understand it, but like his son, it seemed easiest to take out his disappointment by distancing any positive feelings towards me.

On a different front, the Boston Archdiocese sex abuse scandal broke into the news in 2002. And it was in the forefront of the news for the next decade. I was a Catholic and attended church regularly. Religion was an important part of my life and when our family was in crisis, I was praying several times a day. I started feeling queasy during Mass on Sundays. The feeling continued and actually increased in intensity. I was working to protect children and in Church, I was feeling complicit by continuing to support Church leaders who by not taking action, actually put children in harm's way.

I stopped attending church. After about six months, I felt there was a void within me. I felt I was not attending to my spiritual self. For the next two years, I visited other churches, Anglican, Unitarian Universalist to name a few. The Anglican Church I attended reminded me of the Catholic Church back in the 1950s. It was very conservative. The UU church I attended for about a year. I could not disagree with any of their tenets and beliefs. But I didn't feel any passion there within me. It seemed more of an ethic than a religion.

Finally, I landed at an Episcopal Church in a neighboring town. I felt like I had come home. The service was very similar to the Catholic mass, which was comforting. But the message bowled me over. It was all about love and God's forgiveness coupled with a strong social consciousness and a call to fulfill that social calling actively. There was no shame, no focusing in punishment. And an added benefit was they ordained women priests and they were all inclusive. All races and all genders were welcome. I had found the mother lode!

On a parallel tract, after my introduction to AFT (Adoptive Families Together), I joined the support group. It became not only a major support for me in terms of dealing with my family problems, it became a cause I genuinely believed in. I got more involved as the years went on, I was a group leader and led groups such as the ones I had participated in. I went to AFT trainings and gained more knowledge about the adoption experience and tried to keep upgrading my knowledge and expertise. I learned of the seven core issues for adoptees: loss, rejection, guilt, shame, identity, intimacy, and mastery/control. I learned that adoptive parents cannot fix the hurt within their child, but they are needed to facilitate the adoptee's working through the core issues by providing education, understanding, ongoing awareness, and acceptance.

I became a panel speaker at local and then national conferences. I did trainings locally and nationally about how parents should prepare for handling emergencies with their adopted children. I wrote brochures and pamphlets for the organization. Then I became a member of the Board of Directors and later, the President of the Board of Directors. When the organization was struggling with financial viability over a number of years during my term as President, I led the discussion over protecting the organization's future by giving up its autonomy and allowing it to be incorporated into a much larger statewide organization.

While providing education about the adoptive experience, I also presented at conferences for Department of Mental Health and the Department of Social Services. I spoke as not only a mental health professional, but also as a consumer of services of both of their agencies.

My work in AFT and promoting its mission to others was payback for all the help and support I received from them. I did this work concurrently with my other full-time jobs. It was not only very rewarding, but I met some of the most courageous and smart women who had learned to use their pain by turning it to constructive use to bring awareness to others. They helped change the system little by little. We spoke to teachers at teacher-in-services locally. We lobbied legislators; we sponsored bills regarding opening adoption records. This was a grass roots group that accomplished so much.

By 2000, I realized that work at the Mental Health Center was becoming more stressful. As the Director of the crisis team, my job was to ensure that the crisis team provided excellent service to the community by providing quality mental health assessments and treatment plans for the clients we saw both at our office as well as at three community hospitals in our area. I was also responsible for the supervision and training of the crisis clinicians and I was also responsible for their welfare. My boss, who was in charge of my program and several others, was one of the five or six leaders in the agency who made plans for the future and determined what resources would be allocated to various programs. He was heavily influenced by the current CFO (Chief Financial Officer) who had no clinical background.

My boss began hinting and then suggesting that more efficient practices could make the crisis team more cost-effective. I was alarmed when he stated the CFO thought that there was a lot of downtime on the crisis clinicians who worked on the night shift. It was an unpredictable shift. Some nights could be quite slow with five or six phone calls and one evaluation at one of the local hospitals' ED (Emergency Department). But other nights, the phone could be ringing steadily with people in crisis, looking for support or discussing their suicidal ideation. But also, there could be calls from all three EDs stating they needed crisis clinicians to come to their ED to evaluate whether a psych client in the ED was safe to go home with a follow-up plan or needed to be hospitalized in a psychiatric hospital.

o the present is not nearly as precise as his earlier life, sis clinicians could be doing data entry work for other departments during slow times. This was not in any crisis clinician job description. And crisis clinicians considered themselves mental health professionals with a specific skill set in judging and evaluating psychiatric emergencies for safety. It was an insult to their expertise to expect them to do data entry work. I told my boss clearly that I was adamantly opposed to this suggestion. But I could see the handwriting on the wall, so I began to alert my clinicians that change was afoot and to think of their futures and plan accordingly. I did the same for myself. I updated my resume and put it online.

About a month after I posted my resume, I received a call from a headhunter. She said she was located in the Midwest, but she placed executives in New England. She said she had read my resume and thought she could find me a better job. She asked my desired salary range, which I told her.

Then she said she would be back in touch with me. Two weeks later, she called to say she had two possibilities. One was a job as a Nurse Manager at a community hospital just outside of Boston. She asked if she could present my resume to them. I gave her the okay and then she related the way things progressed. First, if they were interested, I would be contacted for a phone screening interview to see if I was an appropriate candidate to bring in for a face-to-face interview.

She felt strongly that I would hear from them, so her next advice was about the phone interview. "You need to stand for the interview; it will make you come across as more assured and confident. And you need to smile as you are giving your responses to the questions. That will make you seem approachable and friendly." She went on to say that I needed to rehearse and I should stand in front of the mirror with a phone and smile while I was talking. *Okay, I thought to myself, but she's the expert here not me.* I rehearsed and my voice did seem softer when smiling.

I did get a call from the Site Director of Nursing and after a thirty-minute phone interview, I got through phase one and was asked to come in for an interview with her and her boss, the Director of Nurses (DON). Again, advice from the head hunter: get your hair done, your nails done, buy a new two-piece outfit, either a suit or a dress and matching jacket.

Interview one went well. I liked both the Site Director and the DON. They asked a lot of questions that I felt were perceptive. They wanted my management style, how I dealt with conflict and with problematic employees. How often did I meet with my staff, how hands-on was my approach? How big was my budget and how many people reported to me? They stated that they actually had two open positions—one as Nurse Manager for an Adult Psychiatric Unit and one for a Child Psychiatric Unit. Both units were locked units. To my surprise, I found myself stating that I would be able to do either position, but my preference was for the Child Unit and I discussed my avocation and my work in AFT.

At this point, they began to explain the challenges I would be faced with in the Child position. The unit had undergone many administrative changes with a number of staff having left en masse in the past year. More importantly, there was one staff person on the unit who was very strong and had posed long standing problems for the unit. I said I felt I was up to that challenge, because my primary goal was to provide the best services for children and their families and anything that tried to undermine that goal would need to be dealt with.

The last question I was asked was salary range. I gave them my response and they said they had thought of a salary $10,000 or less than that. I said I would be unable to accept that as this job entailed an extensive commute, which would result in long hours. They replied that they thought they could come up with a package I would like if things progressed positively.

I left there two hours later feeling good. I was excited and once home, I went online to print up articles on child inpatient care. But I heard nothing. One week went by, then two, then three, and I became discouraged that they must have given the job to someone else. The headhunter checked in and I told her that I had no word after I thought things had gone well. She called the Site Director and called me back. She said that they still were interested in me, but there were some problems on their end that had to be worked out.

Six weeks after my first interview, I was asked to come back to meet with several people, which included the Chief of the Psychiatry Department and the Assistant Chief of the Child Psychiatry Department. Following that, I was to meet with two Nurse Managers from other psych units within the hospital. I also had a half-hour interview with the Medical Director of the Child Unit and she told me that she was leaving in six-weeks' time. She gave me her ideas on what my challenges would be. At the end, I met with the Site Director Mary. These interviews lasted the entire morning. Again, I thought the interviews went well. The only person I could not read was the Assistant Chief of the Child Psychiatry Department. He was friendly, but I did not get the warm vibes from him that I had received from everyone else.

Again, I heard nothing after this interview. I started to have doubts about this hospital, but it was counterbalanced by a feeling that had steadily been growing within me. I felt an affinity to this position. I had not been successful in my efforts to help my troubled son, and here was a job where I could help many children and their families. I knew firsthand all the obstacles to getting help. I knew that explosive children were the most challenging and most misunderstood. I could do something here. I wanted this job badly.

Another two weeks, and I was asked to come back for a third interview, which would be a group interview with some staff of the unit itself. Okay, another obstacle to overcome. I made some copies of some of the articles I had been reading about practices on child units, what worked and what didn't. Mary met with me first to go over the group interview. She saw my printed articles and said: "Keep those for later, for after, you have gained their trust. Right now, they are not feeling trustful or appreciated with all the changes in staff the unit has gone through." She gave me a thumbnail sketch of who she thought might be present for the interview.

The group interview comprised about five or six people, which included a nurse who had worked on the unit a long time, a mental health worker who had worked on the unit for the last year, a social worker, and a psychologist. They were looking for someone who was going to stay, not use the job as a stepping-stone. They were blunt in their disillusionment with the administration who they did not feel was listening to them that the constant exiting of staff had destabilized the unit and it had no cohesion. I assured them, that if I got the job, I was there 'to hang my hat'.

This time, I did not have long to wait. Within days, Mary called and I was officially offered the job. In three weeks, I would be undertaking a major endeavor and I believed that everything I had been through had led me to this path.

From this point on, my life descended on two divergent paths coexisting side by side. There was my family life occurring with Mark, I growing more distant and eventually divorcing and Mark Tomas now in his twenties and criminally involved. But this second path, this new endeavor became my life's work. I felt it was what God had put me on this earth to accomplish. Yet, hand and hand with this new focus and clarity of purpose to make life better for challenged children and their families, my role as a mother was bittersweet. I was so proud of Beth and Andy and their ability to grow into adults, make mistakes, and learn from them. But my heart ached for Mark Tomas who now was an adult and traveling down a criminal and violent road. All the efforts to secure help, the raised hopes that this or that program would be the saving grace had not resulted in positive change. The impression that progress was being made was only an illusion and was followed by learning of drug use and violence.

Several years into this job, I made another major change in this phase of my life. I went back to school in my late 50s, at the age of 58 to be exact! I attended a Nursing Leadership meeting at the hospital and someone sent around a brochure on the LEND program to bring back to the unit to see if any of the nursing staff were interested. The program was funded by a grant from National Institute of Health, Maternal/Child Health Division. It was co-sponsored by Suffolk University, UMASS Medical School, and the Eunice Kennedy Shriver Center. The LEND initials stood for Leadership Excellence in Neuro-Developmental Disabilities.

It was a year course for the LEND certificate and taking six additional courses at Suffolk University resulted in a Masters in Heath Administration. I applied to the program two days from the deadline. I was called for an interview with the Medical Director of the program. One week later, I received a letter of acceptance. The group was small: me, (a psychiatric nurse), a pediatrician, an audiologist, two physical therapists, a speech pathologist, an Occupational therapist, and a psychologist. The program suggested we reduce our workloads to under thirty hours a week. That was not possible for me. The program was fulltime on Thursdays and half-day on Fridays. I worked longer on Mondays, Tuesdays, and Wednesdays, plus I was on call 24/7.

Despite the very long hours for that year and a half, it was an exhilarating experience. I felt like my mind grew by ten years. The courses were aimed at training us as leaders, providing us with skills to be able to influence our respective professional fields for the betterment of children. We were taught how to influence policy makers, how to lobby to influence lawmakers, and we were taught to look at how change was made in other countries. The experience included a trip to Washington, DC to meet with lawmakers regarding pending legislation affecting services for children. We learned how to succinctly make our point using facts and summarizing in five minutes. We also took a trip to Ireland and looked into services provided there depending on our fields of interest.

I visited a community mental health program and a psychiatric hospital for children and met with the program directors. They explained how their services were provided and I answered their questions regarding child psychiatric units and the use of medication in the US. I received my LEND Certification at the end of that year. And three months before my sixtieth birthday, I received my Masters in Health Administration! The only person who would have been affected by my even longer hours at work and school would have been Mark, as the children, now grown were out of the home.

Beth was at college and only home for holidays and summer. Mark and I were already living separate lives within the house. But even despite that, I think he was proud of my endeavor.

Chapter 20
2000 – 2013: Opening Our Arms: Making Change Happen

I had started my new job in March, 2000 at the Child Assessment Unit, and I started with much enthusiasm. I felt ready for this challenge. I had taken the job with the hope of being able to do something worthwhile for children. I had ample quantities of energy and even more of passion and I was ready for something important. I had seen firsthand in my own life that services for children were sorely lacking. I had lots of thoughts and opinions on the way care should be provided to children and their families. I felt up to this task. The unit was housed within a community hospital and was on the seventh floor. It had thirteen beds and served children aged three to thirteen. It was a locked unit.

I saw my first task as identifying which staff seemed to operate in a manner consistent with my values about the care of children. I also wanted to know who was competent, but more importantly, I wanted to know who was curious and wanted to learn. I also needed to identify who would be my challenges. Who did I think would become stumbling blocks in the months ahead as we started down a road to dramatically change the way care was provided to children on psychiatric units.

By the end of six weeks on the job, I had already developed a tremendous appreciation for the nurses and counselors working on the unit. They cared for the children twenty-four hours a day, seven days a week. Decisions made by the clinicians were often played out on the unit. Kids would receive bad news, such as hearing that they would not be going home but to a residential program, or they would have an upsetting family meeting. Some would disclose to their therapist some horrible experience that they had been through and then they would return to the unit.

The overwhelming emotions that had been stirred up would often result in explosions on the unit. Frequently, the staff had no heads up, no warning that Johnny was in for a tough time. The staff were left with the aftermath and with an expectation that they were to keep order at all times. They had a limited set of tools with which to manage a group of kids who had been hospitalized, because they were unable to control their behavior and were deemed 'too dangerous' for the community at this point in time. At its worst, the fear of any psychiatric unit was that of several kids exploding at once and the contagion effect taking over the unit.

I had sensed in the staff an undercurrent of everyone anticipating a worst-case scenario. It was easy to imagine that if enough close calls had occurred, or if staff members were being assaulted on a regular basis, the result would be a group of people who were hyper-alert and hyper-vigilant. They were looking to stomp out any sparks of smoldering emotional distress. The first serious assault occurred within two months of arriving, and I used this as the spark for us to think about doing things differently.

The assault resulted in a sweet, young, Irish female counselor being cold-cocked in the face by a nine-year-old boy resulting in a broken nose. She was taken to the Emergency Department (ED) and then given paid leave for two weeks. When she returned, we had a unit debriefing. Here the staff were free to admit to their fears and concerns about their safety on the unit. They also voiced their anger with the hospital management and stated they felt no support coming from the administration.

They interpreted this lack of support as the 'powers above' tacitly complying with the assumption that they would get hurt and it was just part of the job. I commiserated with them and told them I did not expect them to get hurt, that their welfare was as important to me as that of the children. I also told them that I would fight for resources we needed as they were identified. On another level, I thought this is where the real work needs to be done. We need to understand what motivated this boy to assault her. If we didn't understand why, we couldn't help him. And hadn't that been my experience—I was searching all of my son's early life to find experts who could help me with Mark Tomas's anger with no success despite lots of therapists and programs and meds.

For the next couple of months, I did a lot of observing staff interacting with children on the unit and assessed their skills and their temperament. I slowly introduced into our staff meetings, which occurred weekly, the practice of looking at how the unit handled different situations and opened discussions up to question if we were doing things correctly. And then we raised the possibility that we could be interacting with the children in a different way. I asked the staff to develop a perspective of viewing situations under the lens of 'how would I like my child or relative to be treated' in this or that situation.

In my first years as Nurse Manager, I had a Medical Director, who was also questioning traditional practices in the management and assessment of children. For those first few years, we were a good team. He was a support in working together with me especially when our changing from traditional psychiatric practices was being questioned by both the Psychiatry Department hierarchy and the Hospital Administration.

We capitalized on this assault event to bring us together to begin to look at our procedures and protocols. They were developed and expanded every time an adverse event occurred to ensure 'safety'. I encouraged questioning of our practices and exploring if they actually did what they had been intended to do. I asked directly: "Do you feel safe? Have these procedures made the unit safer?" The overwhelming response was no. The unit felt less safe. I shared with the staff that my thought was that the children we served by and large were victims of trauma. But they were not alone; the staff themselves were victims of trauma based on the assaults on them and the number of restraints and seclusions in which they had participated.

I worked hard to create a climate where questioning current practices was okay and I openly aired my questions with the staff. I went out on the proverbial limb. I was risking people calling into question my sanity, my training, and my competence. In my heart, I felt that although this was risky, it was a lesser risk than not questioning. That, I felt, would result in one of missed opportunities to grow and change. I was able to back up my assertions that the unit was less safe as the result of all the protocols they had developed. We had clear statistics that the level of violence had increased as more rules and consequences were put in place. I offered that we had nothing to lose by looking at things in a different way. Over the course of several months, staff meetings focused on change having the potential to make things a lot better for the kids and the staff.

I needed to find a philosophy or approach that we could adopt together as a group and build upon that philosophy a unit structure to support us in caring for the children we served. I had one of those 'ah ha' moments. I remembered back to a training I had gone to at my last job. It was a presentation to local high school teachers and mental health professionals working with kids. It was a very jaded and frustrated audience and they felt that their city schools were out of control.

The speaker was Ross Greene Ph.D. He discussed his method of evaluating kids' challenging behaviors and his method of dealing with these children. His method was called Collaborative and Proactive Solutions. He was able to win over this highly skeptical audience. He didn't gloss over aggressive behaviors, but he felt that in order for the child to respond non-aggressively, you had to understand what was driving the behavior. Not only did it spark a fire within me, looking beneath the surface was what I had been seeking in professionals throughout Mark Tomas's childhood and adolescence.

He asked everyone not to describe the meltdowns that they witnessed with a child but to look further back in time, to find the underlying cause for the child's building frustration. He believed that if you could learn all that was possible about what was driving the child to become frustrated and then explosive, you would be able to use that knowledge to teach a child the skills that child needed so that he/she could succeed. And if the child was succeeding, then there would be little cause for frustration and an impending explosion.

This was the kind of approach I thought the staff would accept. It smacked of their reality. It was real and it spoke of explosive behavior—exactly the behavior that was part and parcel of our daily experience. It also was solution-focused. One of the doctors on the unit who was about to leave told me she knew Ross Greene and that she would put me in touch with him. He agreed to meet with the Medical Director and me on the unit. The proposition we proposed was that he could use us and our locked psychiatric unit to teach us his CPS method. We would be his first locked psychiatric facility to try this out. It would be a win-win for all of us.

This knowledge was too late for my son, but I thought of all the other children we served. And I held out hope that we could change lives if we found a method or approach in managing very challenging behaviors.

For the next year 2002, we held group supervision sessions twice a week, learning from Ross and his associate. His approach led us to become detectives observing a child's frustration and learning what cognitive deficits were driving the frustration. For each child, that might be different and for many children, there were a myriad of deficits co-occurring. Children on our unit routinely experienced trauma and that left them with a constant state of anxiety that blended itself to frequent misperceptions. Many of our children had difficulties with attention, difficulties with mood regulation, had social skills deficits. We also had kids that were concrete thinkers. Things were either black or they were white; they saw no grey areas. These kids were quite rigid in their thinking and they had extreme difficulty with any change in their routine. Many of the children on the unit had language difficulties, either receptive or expressive or even worse—they had both.

We developed skills to identify these vulnerable areas in the kids we treated. Once we had identified these deficits, we could prioritize a treatment plan that addressed these areas and from this help stabilize them. Ross provided us with a structured approach in dealing with kids as they were beginning to become frustrated. As we began to use his approach, it was scary. We had to begin to learn these skills from our 'in-the-moment' interactions with the children. I believed that I needed to be out there in the forefront giving this approach a try. I knew how to pretend to be calm. I had experience with my son in acting 'as if' I was not scared. I knew how to pretend to have confidence and to be in control in heated situations.

I used that experience to be out in the forefront. I encouraged my coworkers to do the same, "We need to pretend like we know what we are doing until we really do know what we are doing." Ross' model stemmed from his basic assertion: 'Kids do well if they can'. From that basic assumption followed that if a kid was not doing well, it was because he did not know how. It was the adult's job to find out why the child was not doing well and then to teach the child the skills he needed to do well.

So that became our unit mantra and we kept it in our minds in all our interactions with the children. Over and over, we would say: "Remember, kids do well if they can!"

We brought our successes and our failures to each supervision session. That first year was exciting and challenging. A big part of the challenge was those staff persons who were not buying in to this approach. We had asked all the staff to buy in to this approach for a solid six months. There was a core group who were willing to jump in like I was to give this a full-hearted try. Then there was about one-third of the staff, who suspended judgment but held back and watched to see if we were making progress before they jumped in. There was another third of the staff who actively undermined our attempts.

This group was primarily nurses, many with a lot of years of experience. They were entrenched in the belief that to keep the unit safe, it was necessary to impose a rigid structure for kids who had no inner control. 'Keep the unit safe'. It was their contra-mantra. Every return to the old rules and consequences was justified as 'the unit was unsafe'. There was much complaining about my methods and our approach behind my back. There was also one milieu counselor, who took upon himself the role of the 'unit enforcer' and felt he had to make sure the women on the unit were the safe, despite the fact that no woman had asked for his protection.

A few nurses went as far as to call fellow nurses at home and encourage them to find an excuse not to come in for their shift as 'the unit is unsafe, it is too dangerous to come in'. There was the 'primary underminer'—she was the person I had been warned about in my interviews. She was a strong force to be contended with. She had her masters in clinical psychiatric nursing and touted that degree as evidence of her expertise and supreme authority among nursing staff. She had a high degree of indirect power. She spoke frankly to me, "I was here long before you came and I'll be here long after you leave!" There were occasions where I would leave for the day and she was the charge nurse for the evening shift. Staff would report to me the next day that as soon as I closed the unit door behind me, she would turn to the staff and state, "You may have done things her way before, but now we are doing things my way."

This nurse and her friend (another long-time nurse) wrote letters of complaint to the Department of Mental Health and the Board of Nursing. This brought things to a head. The Department of Mental Health's Head of Nursing Licensure contacted my boss, Mary, and stated though they were in support of my efforts, the hospital needed to determine if I had the support of the staff on the unit. The Board of Nursing stated they would await the decision of the Department of Mental Health. After discussion with my boss, we decided to plan for a special staff meeting with a special invitation to the two nurses who had written the letters. We let everyone know that this would be their opportunity to share their thoughts and have a say directly to my boss, the site manager, and to the Director of Nursing.

The special invitation to the two nurses was needed as the 'primary underminer' rarely attended our weekly supervision. But she would sign the written notes I would type out and post in the Nurse's Station. We scheduled the meeting three different times based on one or the other nurse claiming a conflict with the time offered for the meeting. Finally, one of the nurses said they had no intention of attending regardless of when it was held. The staff reported to me that they wanted to go forward with the meeting with our administrators. I was in a quandary as what to do going forward. But my boss related that the Director of Nursing agreed that I should to go ahead and schedule the meeting and that she would be there to hear everyone's thoughts and opinions. I planned the meeting and bought candy and cookies, soda and water for the staff.

I was astounded at the turnout. Over 85% of the staff showed up and participated. They had devised a schedule to take turns freeing up the staff on the unit so that everyone had a say. I was so moved and it proved to be our 'tipping point'. Every staff member spoke up. Even the most shy and quiet employees spoke proudly about what we were accomplishing. Each person around the conference table and lining the perimeters of the room discussed their individual journeys from initial skepticism to some beginning successes to a feeling of pride and accomplishment.

They spoke of being unable to imagine going back to the way things were done before. They stated as a group that they were wholly involved in this effort and they embraced it as their own achievement. They spoke of their freedom in being released from the role of being enforcers. They spoke of their increased sense of job satisfaction. They also shared their personal pride and reward at being able to help a child and being able to show affection to children who had not known what normal healthy affection looked and felt like. They also spoke out about the two naysayers and said that they were the problem on the unit, constantly trying to thwart our efforts and outright escalating the children with their rigid approach.

The administrators were impressed with the outpouring of support and when the meeting was relayed to the DMH, they too were pleased. They stated that no further action needed to be taken and they would relay that to the Board of Nursing. This event served as a further bonding point for our team. I felt so fortunate to have been blessed with these very talented and special people for whom I worked.

One further incident stood out as the clash in values between our old values and culture, and the new ones we were creating. I thought of this as my 'high noon' moment. We had a twelve-year-old girl on the unit, Jakira, who had learned she would not be returning home from the unit. Instead, she would be staying with us until a residential placement could be found. She had spent a large part of the previous week stating over and over that she wanted to be home for her thirteenth birthday. Unfortunately, that was not going to happen and she had been told she would be on the unit for her birthday. When the day arrived, her mom brought in a big tray of homemade cupcakes for us to distribute at her daughter's birthday party later in the afternoon. Jakira had witnessed her mother dropping off the cupcakes.

At lunch, Jakira was in a very irritable mood. She opened her lunch tray and yelled: "I'm not eating this shit!" She proceeded up to the lunch counter and in a very demanding voice, said, "I want one of my cupcakes now." You can already guess who was the nurse behind the lunch counter in the kitchen. (To paint this picture clearly, you need to know that we had had major discussions about food and the role it played on the unit. We had made a group decision that rules about food was no longer of primary importance. We were a psych unit and teaching life lessons was not our task. We did not feel struggling over food was part of our mission.) The nurse replied: "You need to eat your lunch first."

Jakira replied: "I want one of my god dammed cupcakes!"

This nurse escalated the situation further by replying: "They are not your cupcakes. Your mother brought them in to the staff for your party later this afternoon. You can't have them now."

Jakira was now enraged and slammed her lunch tray on the counter with a bang. "Give me one of my cupcakes!" she yelled. The lunchroom became quiet. The rest of the staff were poised around the room and in front of it.

I approached the nurse and said quietly, "I thought we had decided in group supervision that food was not an enforceable rule that we wanted to be involved with."

She replied, "We have to keep some semblance of good nutrition on the unit. Besides, the cupcakes are for her party later this afternoon."

I then replied: "It's her birthday. Give her the damn cupcake."

She was now visibly upset and she got the cupcake tray and slammed it down on the counter. She turned to me and said, "You want her to have the cupcake, then you give it to her." She left the kitchen and went to the staff lounge.

I took a cupcake, placed it on a paper plate, and said, "Happy Birthday, Jakira," and followed it up with a hug and a kiss. The staff observing this event gave me silent support with 'high fives' and hand signals.

At the end of a year's time, we had lost one-third of the nursing staff and almost twenty percent of the milieu counselors. A number of the milieu counselors left to further their education, which is an expected outcome. As difficult as it was to lose a portion of the staff, it needed to happen. The staff would come to me and state that the negative staff were undermining their efforts and their approach, and were not only confusing the kids, but their approach was escalating them. The nurses who were undermining our moving forward, all resigned and new hires were interviewed and trained to join with us in our endeavors.

Undertaking this huge project bonded the staff together. We were changing the structure of the unit step by step, mastering new skills, seeing results, and building a new unit culture. The regulating agencies of DMH and DCF, although they received a few more complaints from a few of the staff, were supportive of us and wanted us to succeed. By the end of the second year, word was beginning to spread that we were doing something different. The DMH began to make requests for us to take very difficult children who were being placed in numerous restraints in other institutions within the state. They were also referring staff of different programs within the state to check out what we were doing.

We began to invite staff from various programs who were calling to ask questions, spend a day on the unit with us to see us in action. I also started presenting at state conferences and told them of our experience.

Four years in, and we began to say that: "CPS started as a method, then it became a unit culture and it evolved to be an ethic." It now felt morally wrong to impose traditional practices on vulnerable kids. Everyone who had been part of a traditional milieu structure was feeling badly about actions they may have been part of in the past. We had to forgive ourselves for things we had done before we knew any better and before we knew there was another way.

We did wonderful things on this unit. We created 'OPEN HOURS' for parents and grandparents. This meant they could visit when they wanted as often as they wanted. Traditional units had very limited visiting. Usually for an hour in the afternoon or evening. It was very difficult for working parents to visit. Either they were at work or they were at home cooking dinner for their other children. We encouraged parents to help settle their children at bedtime. We allowed parents to sleep over, especially in the beginning before they and their child got to know and trust us.

We had children sleep on their mattress in the hallway in view of night staff on the first day of admission. Some children who were afraid of dark bedrooms were allowed to sleep in the hall nightly and we gradually transitioned them to the bedroom. We encouraged parents to come on the unit and watch us in action interacting with their child and other children. We encouraged their questions and the staff taught them how to begin the problem-solving process with their child. We shared what we learned about each child with the parents and suggested strategies to avoid explosions.

We worked diligently to avoid coercive interventions and decreased to nearly zero our incidences of seclusion and physical restraints. This was an amazing accomplishment.

We tailored a child's schedule on the unit based on our assessment of what we thought they could handle at any point in time. We did not force them to attend groups before they were ready, which would only exacerbate a meltdown.

Most psychiatric units had a 'hands off' policy. We gave ample amounts of hugs and praise to children. Even the most seasoned, cynical child was able to see within twenty-four hours that we were doing something different here. They could let their armor down. We watched guarded, heavily defended, and aggressive children warm up, relax, and open up. We saw them respond to hugs, positive touch, and positive remarks pointing out the wonderful qualities we observed in them. We saw white children initially fearful of black staff respond to the affection bestowed upon them, and these children were able to let go of stereotypes.

They would actually gravitate to that particular staff person. We witnessed black children, initially wary and restrained in the close presence of white staff, lose their reservations and delight in wraparound hugs and praise from nurturing staff. We observed latency-age children, who believed they were too old for hugs and expected little, come around and run up to staff with their arms open wide. We unabashedly opened our arms wide to embrace the children we served, and we saw the results in the delighted smiles of the children who came to us discouraged, defeated, and scared. We saw many of them leave us a little more hopeful, a little stronger, and beginning to heal.

We had a 'Random Acts of Kindness' competition where we posted a large poster with 100 blocks of space. Every time a staff observed a child acting kindly to another child, their initials were posted in one of the blocks. When we had all 100 spaces filled with the children's initials, we celebrated with a big pizza party with soda, cake, and music and dancing.

I purchased a large supply of rollerblades and we ran groups teaching all the children to rollerblade. Our unit had a large long hallway, so there was plenty of room for the kids to skate up and down. If a child learned nothing else, they left the unit with increased confidence knowing how to rollerblade.

We also recognized the staff who were going the extra mile in their attempts to master CPS and a humane and healing environment. We had sheets in the staff lounge entitled: 'Caught you doing something good!' Staff members were encouraged to report their observations of other staff having positive interactions with the children, other staff members, and interventions that helped a child deescalate preventing a meltdown. At weekly staff meetings, I would read out the sheets praising various staff for their actions the previous week.

We met with parents often and staff were encouraged to interact with parents, share with them what we had learned about their child. We also shared this information with schools and made recommendations regarding their placement and Individualized Educational Plans.

One poignant memory for me was our experience with Antonio. He was a twelve-year-old boy admitted to the unit for 'out of control behavior at home and at school'. He had a history of school truancy also. His older brother was in juvenile detention. His mom was an overwhelmed single mom who was trying to manage two acting out boys, poverty, impending homelessness, and her own terminal diagnosis of AIDS. We tried to engage her, but initially phone calls were not returned and then we learned her phone had been disconnected. She gave us several different phone numbers, but when we called them, the persons answering the phone reported that she did not live there. She believed that her children did not know of her diagnosis.

As we got to know Antonio, we learned that his out of control behavior was due to his overwhelming worry and anxiety knowing his mother was dying. He had heard her talking about it on the phone and he was aware her mental status was changing. When she was on the unit, he acted parentified, cuing her and worrying about her responses to us. He was very protective of her. Our work involved getting Antonio's mom to trust us so that we could help her with the services she would need in the community. It also involved letting her know that Antonio's explosiveness was his response to dealing with his grief and anxiety over knowing that she was dying.

We needed her to confide in us that she was homeless so we could arrange for housing with the proper agency. We stressed how important she was in Antonio's life and asked her to spend as many nights with him as she could while he was on our unit. He asked to sleep in the hall and he asked if she could sleep beside him at the end of the hall. We gave them two mattresses to set up and they put them side by side. He fell asleep with a smile on his face, cradled in her arms. When I was asked by a few staff if this was alright, my answer was that it was better than alright. She was giving him the gift of warm memories that he could carry with him after she was gone.

This was diametrically opposed to my experience with Mark Tomas's hospitalizations. It was everything that did not happen with my son, but it was happening now with all these children and their parents.

As time went on, I spoke at National and International Conferences. I invited staff from all over the country to come to our unit and observe. I also started consulting with other psychiatric hospitals who were interested in moving to a more humane structure. We sometimes had as many as eight staff observing us from a different hospital or program. Our visitors came from as far as Australia, England, and Canada and from Montana, Texas, Ohio, North Carolina, Arkansas, Virginia, Rhode Island, Vermont, Maine, New York and Kansas City. The work became larger than just one unit. Some visiting staff were with us for three days at a time. We were passing the work on to other units who were striving to develop their own humane practices.

In 2006, I published *Opening Our Arms: Helping Troubled Kids Do Well*. The book documented all the steps we had taken to create a more humane environment where children could be better understood, cherished, appreciated, and loved. And we did it through innovation, not by following standardized practice. All of the total preoccupation with evidenced-based practice leaves little room for change. Innovators do not have evidence-based research. They are starting out believing that current practice that is evidence-based has its own bias. Researchers trying to move the curve forward—need to seek out innovative programs and begin doing research studies with these programs.

Our Unit was co-recipients for the Gold Award for Service Excellence and Innovation for Psychiatric Services from the American Psychiatric Association in 2003. In 2009, I received the American Psychiatric Nursing Association Award for Innovation and Leadership. As I was retiring, the Massachusetts Department of Mental Health presented me with The State of Massachusetts Award in recognition of 'your extraordinary commitment to improve the care of children'.

I had developed a definition of child-centered care that worked for me: 'Child-centered care recognizes the inherent rights of every child, is respectful, and believes care should be nurturing. It is aimed at teaching and providing choices that are based on a child's individual needs. Decisions about care are collaborative and involve the child in decision-making to the greatest extent possible based on age and the child's developmental ability. Child-centered care recognizes that honesty and openness are prerequisites to the development of a trusting relationship where collaboration and decision-making can take place.'

This was my life's work. I was able to channel all things that had not happened for Mark Tomas and use my disappointment, frustration, and knowledge of what was wrong with services to create, with the help of great coworkers, a wonderful place for troubled children.

I remained at this special place until July, 2013. After pouring my heart and soul into this job, I retired. It was my hope that the work for improving services to children would go on, especially on the units where I consulted and the staff from all the units that had visited us. I did hear from one of my co-workers a year after I retired that she and few others on the unit would say to each other in challenging situations: "Now, what would Kathy do?"

One of the immediate benefits upon retiring was the opportunity to have my body relearn uninterrupted sleep. This is no small perk. For my last two jobs, I was required to carry a beeper and be on call 24/7. As Program Director for the crisis team during my term, when any clinician was sending home a person they had evaluated who was considered high-risk, the decision had to be reviewed by me. I was also called when a clinician was not sure in determining the outcome of the emergency evaluation. That meant that frequently, I was called at night, not once, but sometimes two or three times a night. As Nurse Manager of the unit, I was on call to my staff when there were problems on the unit but more frequently for sick calls for upcoming shifts.

I would have to review the current state of the unit and make decisions giving the ok to authorize overtime to staff who volunteered to work a double shift. Other times, I would make arrangements to move staff around shifts for better coverage. Managing a staff of thirty-five people or so covering all three shifts seven days a week meant that I was called at night and late in the evening when sick calls came into the unit. I was also called for advice when the evening shift or the night shift were having problems with children having meltdowns. The result was that I was called frequently at night both week nights and weekend nights. My body now had the opportunity after twenty-six years to learn to sleep through the night.

Another benefit of retiring was a major decrease in daily stress. As stressful as the unit could become at times, that was nothing compared to the bureaucratic stress of working for a large organization with many bosses. I was accountable in the Nursing Department to my immediate boss and to the Director of Nursing. The hospital was a Harvard-affiliated teaching facility, so the psychiatric units were also overseen by the Harvard-affiliated Psychiatry Department and their chiefs. In addition, budget issues and management came under the oversight of the Chief Financial Officer and his department. During my time at the Child Assessment Unit, the hospital's financial picture shifted dramatically and that turn of events impacted greatly my autonomy in running a unit based solely on clinical decision-making.

We had been a 'safety net' hospital, which meant we were one of few hospitals in the state who would take the uninsured. As Massachusetts switched to a health care system that was the forerunner of the Affordable Care Act, our hospital and the few other 'safety net' hospitals suffered under this transition. Our allotment of state funding decreased and once the uninsured population became insured, those hospitals that had previously refused the uninsured now were clamoring for them. My observations were that when the financial picture gets tenuous, the financial officers have more say over how budgets are allocated and spent and this finally drips down into clinical areas. Clinical decisions are no longer sacrosanct and the pressure builds and this stress effects the power brokers in clinical areas and departments.

I also had observed from my consulting with other university-based medical hospitals that universities that had both medical Schools and nursing schools have much better collaborative relationships between the two departments. Our hospital had a more separated structure between Psychiatry and Nursing. We were separate silos in many ways, which frequently created tension. Couple that organizational structure with my strong personality and determination to create a more humane environment for children, come 'hell or high water' and you can imagine that the traditional psychiatry department was often less than thrilled with me and my influence.

And I did, in all honesty, push those boundaries. Because in my heart, I believed in what we were doing and I put my heart and soul into making it happen. I loved my work and the opportunity to accomplish what I did, but I was not going to miss the bureaucracy or the need to defend what we were doing and having to protect our gains. I hoped the staff would carry on as best they could and that they would be able to retain a lot of what we had created.

In my estimation though, I thought the impact on what we had achieved would likely live on more fully in some of the places that had visited us and involved me in consulting on their units. I could see the fervor and the total buy in some of these institutions by both psychiatry and nursing on an equal basis. I hope that they will be my lasting legacy.

Chapter 21
2014 – 2019: Life After the Event

It is now over four years later from the day on which I had received that earth-shattering phone call. As a court case, this has been very complicated and also complex. There have been multiple motions filed, numerous continuances, and a host of people becoming involved in the case and then exiting. Mark Tomas has refused to answer any questions about what occurred in the home. He, in fact, became verbally abusive and threatening to his first public defender after he had made several attempts to get Mark Tomas to discuss what happened. The Public Defender asked to be dismissed from the case. The same situation occurred with his second court-appointed defender.

Then Mark Tomas actually began yelling and threatening to the judge in court. The judge refused to be intimidated and did not recuse himself. The third court-appointed attorney tried to obtain history on Mark, which might have some bearing on his unusual behavior. He seemed able to conduct a normal conversation about inconsequential topics. But any attempt at discussing the case itself resulted in Mark becoming agitated and he would start yelling, cursing, and make threatening remarks. This attorney, in the one telephone conversation I had with him, related that his opinion was that Mark Tomas has a specific delusion around the murder.

Since the charges were so serious, murder one being a capital offence, the judge was reluctant to have Mark defend himself. Any verdict with Mark Tomas defending himself was likely to be questioned and appealed. The judge ordered a forensic psychiatric evaluation to be completed. He was remanded to Bridgewater State Hospital for an evaluation to be completed. Mark was kept there for twenty-one days. He refused to talk, so the report to the judge was inconclusive and not helpful. It stated that since he refused to talk, it could not be determined that he was competent or not competent. Mark Tomas was demanding the judge fire the third court-appointed attorney. When this third attorney had called me, I shared my thoughts. My thought was that the only attorney Mark might be willing to tolerate was an attorney who had represented him as a youth. She was the daughter of his adoption therapist and she herself was adopted and her children were transracial—so there was a connection between them on a number of levels.

This recommendation was made by the third attorney since Mark Tomas was demanding that he too be taken off the case. He felt it was only a matter of time before he would be removed from the case. I had shared Mark Tomas's childhood lawyer as a possible workable solution. Initially, when he made this request, the request was denied as there are certain criteria that must be met to represent someone charged with a capital offense in Superior Court. After a number of weeks, the judge and the trial attorney board of overseers determined that this attorney could sit as second chair and another lawyer with the needed experience in capital cases would be the lead chair. Mark's second chair-attorney would lead any discussions with Mark.

Since he was tolerating this attorney yet not cooperating in preparing a defense, another attorney was added as an 'amicus' attorney. This attorney would represent any mental health issues and would report directly to the judge. Mark's behavior was clearly not normal, but he was not overtly psychotic in a consistent manner. This 'amicus' attorney requested a second psychiatric evaluation. A forensic psychologist was appointed to complete this evaluation. Several months later, this expert contacted me. We had a phone call appointment set up the following week.

I think the phone call took place on a Monday morning at 10 am in December of 2016. The expert seemed friendly and tried to put me at ease. He asked questions and I tried to respond as honestly as I could. His questions moved around and were not in chronological order. I think this was intentional. The interview probably took 50 to 55 minutes. I noticed at the end of the interview that I was feeling anxious, and my body temperature seemed to be hot. When I hung up the phone, I became light-headed, dizzy, and was hyperventilating.

My heart appeared to be hammering in my chest. I lowered my head to my lap, took slow, cleansing breaths, and just told myself to stay calm. After a few minutes, my head began to clear, my heart rate slowed, and I was taking deep breaths. I was proud of taking control of my reaction. The result of mastering that unusual anxiety attack was that I had little memory of the entire phone call. It had been almost totally erased from my mind. I did recall that I had shared Mark's first developmental assessment at New England Medical Center Hospital and the report we received. I also remember his asking me if I thought Mark genuinely cared for his brother and sister and I said yes, I believed he really did have positive feelings for them. But all the rest of the interview—it's a blank. Maybe parts of it will slowly come back in time.

A court date was scheduled for late July, 2017. It was my understanding that the July hearing was still dealing with issues around competency. It is possible that the prosecution might ask for another evaluation to be done by one of their appointed experts. I had learned sometime in March that the second forensic evaluation was given to the judge and it too stated the findings were inconclusive.

I did not think that there would be an actual trial date by the end of last year. One complication is the definitions of the mental and legal competency are quite different. Legal incompetency is rarely determined and granted. Such a determination places a person in a forensic psychiatric hospital until such time that he is determined legally competent to stand trial. I learned a third forensic evaluation was done by evaluating documents only and that after the third evaluation, the judge decided to bring the case to trial.

My limited understanding is that murder one and capital murder are essentially the same. There are only seven states where the term capital murder is being used as those seven states use capital punishment (electrocution or lethal injection). The state of Massachusetts does not have capital punishment at this point in time. As it is considered a liberal state, it is unlikely that capital punishment will ever be reinstated. To prove murder one, it must be proved that there was 'premeditation, intention', and that the act was 'done with reckless disregard for human life', which is also 'malice aforethought'. Under specific examples of crimes within the Massachusetts statute, there is one listed for 'armed assault in a dwelling'. I do not know if this is the designation for which the prosecution charged Mark with murder one. It is considered the most serious crime an individual can commit and carries with it a life sentence. I learned at the end of last year that the forth attorney and the second chair were granted their request to be removed as Mark Tomas' court appointed attorneys for 'serious safety concerns'. A fifth attorney has been appointed and this attorney will be given time to get prepared to represent Mark. As I write this now, I have not learned that a new trial date has been set.

What to make of all of this is complicated. We were not perfect parents, but we tried and tried and tried. We did bond with our son and we loved him. He was dealt a bad hand with many inborn challenges to master if he was to succeed and have a productive life. His inability to manage his anger set him up to fail. It also was triggered by constant frustration that tasks were found difficult due to his multiple learning disabilities. He was smart, but he couldn't keep up.

So, the question for me has been: *Was our adopting him in his best interest?* I am a firm believer in adoption and spent many years of my life active in adoption causes and was at one period of my life, the President of the Board of Directors for Adoptive Families Together. I spent years working in this organization fostering better education and understanding of adoption issues. When I look back on our experience and reflect on what has happened, I think there is no easy answer.

I believe that that it is possible that had Mark Tomas been raised within his Mexican heritage, he would have had one less major issue to contend with when he was trying to develop an identity. He might have struggled with and mastered his identity within our family if he did not also have major learning disabilities to overcome. But I think in my heart, having all those issues to contend with and adding transracial identity issues was too much. I also wonder if a PET scan was done, would it show unusual activity in the area of the brain that controls our emotional output. Is there a biological component here also impacting these events? But the bottom line is that our adopting him with the very best of intentions, the desire to have a family, led to unimaginable ***unintended consequences.***

It has now been determined that he is legally fit to stand trial. I have already decided to return to Massachusetts to attend the trial and sit behind his section with the defense. For all his problems and his history of violence, I still remain his mother, a commitment for life. I love him despite my fear of him at times. When a trial date is set, I will steel myself to prepare for it. I continue to pray that he will find God in prison. For years, I have felt that this could be the primary factor in his being able to turn things around. I pray for him daily as I do for his brother and sister. He used to tell me when he was in his late teen years that he did not expect to live beyond his thirty-fifth birthday. He is now thirty-eight, so I still have some degree of hope that he will one day be open to God's presence in his life. My prayers are that he will find peace and a positive purpose at some point.

It does not appear to me at this time that he will ever be free again, which means he will spend the rest of his life either in jail or in a forensic hospital or both. It is just so tragic.

I hope for a fair trial. That does not mean that I wish he not be found guilty. I want it to be a just judgment. Some people may wonder why as a mother, I am not giving him the benefit of doubt. I think my knowledge of his potential for violence and the sometimes-volatile interactions between he and his father led me down the road that says he did this. Also, the prosecutors have told the Regan family that they believe they have an airtight case that only Mark Tomas could have done this act. I also believe that the act itself may have pushed his mind to a place where he genuinely believes he did not do this. He could easily delude himself that this was a drug deal gone badly and this was retaliation. His peer group was criminals and gang members.

There is a high likelihood that we may never know exactly what transpired that late Tuesday night. Mark is the only witness and he is not talking.

Again, I am stating that my finally making the decision not to continue visiting him in prison was made after repeated unsuccessful visits. Mark Tomas would appear uncomfortable in my presence, often not making eye contact, and would make no conversation with me. If I received an answer to a question I asked, it was a one-word answer. I did not feel my visits brought him any comfort—in fact, it looked like just the opposite. It was such a contrast to my observing him relate to his father sitting next to me.

I went away from those visits feeling awful. My heart ached that I could see no positive reaction to my presence. When I did stop my visits, I would send him letters and books, but I never got an answer. I believe my presence stirs something up in him that is unpleasant. There is still a chance that at some point, that may change. His attorney knows how to contact me. I have heard second-hand that Mark Tomas had contact with his biological mother one month before the murder. I don't know any more than that. I don't know if that was the first contact in years or if they had some sporadic or regular correspondence.

I am now in southern Florida, having relocated approximately fifteen hundred miles south of where I spent the majority of my life. My move here was not just the result of a brutal winter that at one point had me homebound for ten days and shoveling for several hours a day consecutively for nineteen days.

Moving to a more hospitable climate seems an appropriate rationale for a woman living alone. And for someone who has now joined the ranks of other baby boomers—we are all securing positions in the senior citizen ranks. No, the underlying motivation for uprooting myself and making this bold move was to find a new place to start over. I viewed moving as a search to find some peace. I desired to find a place that had spaces for me to find minutes of serenity; a new beginning that felt positive. I hoped for a place where it would be easier to nurture myself. I had already adjusted to being alone and had learned to enjoy periods of solitude and reflection. Additionally, I felt that if I didn't take this step now, I would not have the courage to do so at a later point in my life. I had been retired for five years and that adjustment in lifestyle felt completed and positive. I was ready to take on this challenge.

I like my new home and community. I have found spaces that allow me to feel a sense of peace and have found other friends here who are also starting over to one degree or another.

As a mother of three children, I am now released from the responsibilities of providing for their care. They are adults with their own responsibilities and cares. Two of my adult children have successful lives, foremost of which is having the capacity to seek out satisfying, loving relationships with me and with others. Beth did reunite with her biological family and that is a happier tale. But that story belongs to her and is for her to tell, not me. Andy is a father of four children.

My eldest child, Mark Tomas had his own multiple and complex challenges from a very young age. His challenges impacted our family as a whole, but the events of the last four years have been devastating. As I write this and look back on the early years and then reflect on the last twenty years—I still get shook and totally rattled by the catastrophic event that has occurred.

I look back on the early years and remember the intensity of my maternal involvement in trying to identify Mark's early symptoms, his learning difficulties, my trying to understand the source of his anger, the multiple diagnoses, my looking for answers and hoping for solutions. I remember what it felt like to be in the thick of it. I also remember the angst, the holding my breath sensation, that anxious sense of waiting for the axe to fall, the gut-wrenching sensation I felt each and every time the police were at our door.

I also have twenty years of distance over the experiences and events that occurred when our family was young and the events of the twenty years following that influenced how I reacted to developing events in Mark's teen years and then early adulthood as well as the change in our relationships as our challenges continued. I can admit with honesty that looking back on the last twenty years has a different flavor from that of the agonizing rawness of our first sixteen years as a family. When difficult and scary challenges repeat themselves over and over, there is a desensitizing effect that goes with it.

My memory of the events in this period of time from Mark Tomas's high school graduation up to the present is not nearly as precise as his earlier life, which I had documented some twenty-five years ago with precise notes when I was seeking help from experts and agencies. Those notes were written at a time I still had hope that we could turn things around, learn from the past and move on.

How do I come to terms with all that has transpired? How have I survived and am still be able to put one foot in front of the other and keep going? What makes me able to laugh, seek and find peace, and keep engaging with people? How did I end up in the ranks of those found in the 'What bad things happen to good people' sector? Why did I write this memoir with the chance that at some point, it might become public? What makes me resilient? How am I able to feel hope after so many disappointments?

First, coming to terms with all that has transpired is an ongoing process. There is no finality and the trial still lies ahead. What I do know is that coping is an art that requires skills to draw from. And there is a menu of techniques in the coping skills toolbox. For me, a valuable tool has been my ability to compartmentalize. I developed a skill to allow myself to worry only at designated times. This skill developed over time.

When things were in crisis mode, this was not possible. But over the years, I have become adept at setting up structured times to look, feel, and go over what has transpired. Other positive coping skills I utilized included crying, which at times brought tears of relief and the ability to seek comfort. When crying became out of hand in the midst of ongoing crisis, I sought support not only from my friends but also from professionals. I used sublimation techniques to channel psychic energy into acceptable activities. Going hand in hand with this mechanism, I employed post-traumatic growth and used the energy of trauma for good. Overlying all of this was the principle that positive coping also involves spiritual growth and the finding ways of turning the problem into a way to grow spiritually and emotionally.

I used my psychic energy resulting from the pain, anxiety, and disappointments of what had happened with my oldest son to do my life's work; to effect countless children and their families in a positive way that helped their lives. I spread this message to many other facilities open to creating humane environments for children and families. I also was adept at using substitution as a coping strategy. I liked replacing bad things with good things and encouraged others at presentations and consultations to come see us in action and see how their units could be so much better with a more humane approach.

I was honored to be interviewed by a writer for my alma mater, Suffolk University for an article about me and my work published in Suffolk Alumni magazine entitled: 'The Child Whisperer'.

Along with those skills, I have found for me that writing my thoughts down on paper helps me work things through. Writing for me involves problem solving and through the writing process, I find solutions that work for me. In writing the book about our work on the Child Assessment Unit, I was able to document our finding solutions that worked for us and from that process, we developed a sense of conviction that we were on the right path.

When administrators at the hospital were pressuring and questioning our CPS implementation, I worked through my reasoning by writing peer review articles, which I published. They were entitled: *Paradigm Shifts in Inpatient Psychiatric Care of Children: Approaching Child-Centered and Family Centered Care* (Journal of Child and Adolescent Psychiatric Nursing, 2006, Vol 19, n:29–40) and *Trauma Informed Care on an Inpatient Pediatric Psychiatric unit and the emergence of ethical dilemmas as nurses evolved their practice* (Issues in Inpatient Mental Health Nursing, 2010 31:216–222). They were my response to the traditional hierarchy questioning my abandonment of traditional protocols and practice.

I had also written a small article about domestic violence for Advance for Nurses entitled: *When Daddy hits Mommy*, 10/142003 (33) 22–23. That same year, I wrote a short piece for Nursing Spectrum: *Loosening Restraints* (4/5/03, (5) 5) and in Advance for Nurses: *More than Lip Service, Putting the 'child' back in child-centered care* (June 9,2003 Vol 22, p13) I also wrote for AFT, Inc. Educational Pamphlet Series, *'When the going gets tough': Handling a Psychiatric Crisis or Emergency: What to do when you have a crisis on your hands:*1999. Again, for AFT, Inc. Educational Pamphlet Series, *Restraint and Seclusion: What parents need to know*, 2003.

I am present-focused. I do not dwell on a past that I cannot change. I am also future-oriented. I like planning ahead. I like learning new things. I love to read and feel that reading itself is an enriching and expanding process. Reading is learning from other people's experiences, both real and fictionalized. I enjoy spending time with people and I also need 'down time'. I chose my time with people carefully. I seek out friendships with people who I respect and who share similar basic human values. I avoid negativity and complaining. I avoid the 'glass half-empty' viewers and connect with those who see the 'glass half-full'.

I have always loved to cook. It relaxes me and puts my head in a good place. It is also a continuing connection with my mother. My sister and I spent many weekends and holidays learning from my mother. She had a huge repertoire of cookbooks and took on new cooking styles without any anxiety. She was of Irish and English descent, but my father, who was Italian, taught her the basics of Italian cooking and she surpassed him in this area and was the best Italian cook of all our Italian relatives. Living alone, I still plan special meals to cook in the evenings, though I have not learned to cook for one and the most special meals I endeavor could feed at least four people!

I am comfortable in my own skin. I am no longer a work in progress. I am fond of being the boss of me. I value quietness. I have lived alone for a long time and there is a tranquility that comes with living alone. I have become so comfortable with quiet that I find noise disquieting.

I also believe in destiny. And there is some truth to the adage that 'What doesn't kill you makes you stronger'. I do believe that going through very challenging times and emerging out the other end does inure you much like firing clay pottery. In my twenties, I took an adult-education astrology course where we learned to do our own astrological charts both Western and Eastern Astrology. I had seven planets in Scorpio. Fascinating to me at the time was learning from the Eastern astrological interpretation that my chart suggested that this was my final lifetime and that it would be a very challenging one as I would be making up for mistakes in previous lifetimes so that I could evolve out to a higher spiritual plane. But my twenty-something-year-old self could never have imagined what lied before her.

I think I was blessed with a strong emotional core. I was able to avoid being mired down in distress and being solution-focused led me to action and doing something constructive with the life experiences I had been dealt. I come from a long line of strong women. I had the benefit of being raised in a middle-class family where education, religion, social justice, and making the world a better place were valued tenets.

At church, one Sunday, Father Marty Zlatic gave a sermon, which really registered with me. He talked of finding prayer in the 'thin spaces'. I went home and looked up the reference. I found an article by Eric Weiner who described the 'thin spaces' as "locales where the distance between heaven and earth collapses and we're able to catch glimpses of the divine, or the transcendent" or, as I like to call it, the 'Infinite Whatever'. He suspected the phrase was coined by some ancient Celt as they believed Heaven and Earth were only three feet apart. Father Marty described the 'thin spaces' as places where God is more accessible and where a sense of peace is almost tangible. During his sermon, I had an 'aha moment'. I remembered the peace I find in God's beautiful earth and how walking in the woods or on the beach would bring a sense of peace and wonder.

Daily, I look and find the 'thin spaces' in my life; beautiful cloud formations, which here in southern Florida occur daily. 'Thin spaces' are bountiful here with beautiful beaches and wonderful state and local parks such as Green Cay. I find I am in a thin space spending time with old friends whose support is always present and with new friends who enjoy spending time with me. I feel a sense of inner peace most of the time and I worked on developing it in my Tai Chi QI Gong classes. There we learned how to perform different movements and forms that have graceful symmetry with beautiful spiritual meditations that accompany the forms.

My life here is filled with activities and interactions that occupy my days. I have Bella (a five-year-old Italian Greyhound) who adores me and anyone who enters our home. She loves to cuddle and sleep by my side night and day. (She sleeps almost twenty hours a day!) I try to write one or two hours a day several days a week. I enjoy water aerobics, Tai Chi, and I play Canasta with good Canasta buddies three times a week. I participate in a number of the myriad social activities in my community. I have a group of friends, which consists of couples and single women who like to go out to eat together monthly. Bella and I take a long walk early every morning. In the evenings, she relaxes with me as I watch TV or read. I never tire of the beauty of my surroundings and I am blessed to be in a beautiful gated community that looks like a resort.

Being present in the 'thin spaces' enriches my experience. I feel God's presence and I appreciate the gifts I have been given. I recognize my community of friends and feel blessed by friends and relatives that love and support me on the good days and the bad ones also. God's presence in these spaces brings with it the perspective about what is really important.

Why did I write this memoir? The need to work out problems by documenting them and putting words to paper is only one part of the reason behind this memoir. I also thought it would be helpful to my children and their children and maybe even generations beyond that to have a larger view of me as a person. I know that after my mother died, I would find that there were questions I had wished I had asked her about her life and the lives of her relatives.

But that too was just part of my reasoning. Families in crisis still feel a sense of being stigmatized, misunderstood, and of being judged. I wanted to have the courage to tell my story in the hopes of shedding some light on this dilemma and to encourage others to also speak up about the difficulties they faced. I also felt that my story though upsetting shows how even in very trying circumstances, gathering your strengths and using your talents helps your resilience grow. The stronger your resilience, the more you feel empowered and the more in control you are over your life and its trajectory. My story is sad, but it also attests to having hope and overcoming very difficult challenges. Having walked in my shoes, it is impossible to sweat the small stuff. You are forced to alter your perspective from the difficulties you faced to the good you can create for others.

My life has traveled a bumpy road, but I am well. I have loved and been loved. I am ready for what lies ahead and know I will have the support and good wishes of my family and friends. I am blessed.

The End

CPSIA information can be obtained
at www.ICGtesting.com
Printed in the USA
LVHW051100150419
614196LV00014B/207